18.95

INTRODUCING FORMAL METHODS
A Less Mathematical Approach

ELLIS HORWOOD SERIES IN COMPUTERS AND THEIR APPLICATIONS

Series Editor: IAN CHIVERS, Senior Analyst, The Computer Centre, King's College, London, and formerly Senior Programmer and Analyst, Imperial College of Science and Technology, University of London

Series continued at back of book

INTRODUCING FORMAL METHODS

A Less Mathematical Approach

NEVILLE FORD
Senior Lecturer, Chester College

JUDITH FORD
Freelance Computer Programmer

ELLIS HORWOOD
NEW YORK LONDON TORONTO SYDNEY TOKYO SINGAPORE

First published in 1993 by
ELLIS HORWOOD LIMITED
Market Cross House, Cooper Street,
Chichester, West Sussex, PO19 1EB, England

A division of
Simon & Schuster International Group
A Paramount Communications Company

Printed and bound in Great Britain
by Hartnolls, Bodmin

British Library Cataloguing in Publication Data

A catalogue record for this book is available from the British Library

ISBN 0–13–484320–7   (Pbk)

Library of Congress Cataloging-in-Publication Data

Available from the publisher

Table of Contents

Preface

This is a book about Formal Methods. We have written it in the belief that Formal Methods are important and have an increasingly important role to play in Software Development. In this book, we present a discussion of Formal Methods which relies upon little previous knowledge of mathematics. However, in order to set Formal Methods within a practical context, we do assume some knowledge of programming.

There are several works which are widely used in teaching Formal Methods. Jones (1990) and Hekmatpour & Ince (1988) are two existing works to which we have referred extensively. This present work aims to introduce and complement the work covered in these earlier texts rather than to replace it.

Formal Methods have their roots in the desire to write Quality Computer Software. We use this aim as our starting point, and so we begin by discussing the techniques of Software Engineering, since these techniques have been developed with the aim of improving the quality of the software development process.

A consideration of software engineering methods in chapters 1 & 2 leads naturally to an important conclusion: the accuracy with which the *requirements definition* and *requirements specification* may be described lies at the root of improving the quality of software development. Therefore, in chapter 3, we focus on various ways in which the requirements of a system may be described. These *informal* methods can be seen to have some good features but they also display some shortcomings, and in chapter 4 we introduce the first ideas of a more *formal* method of specification.

These ideas are developed thoughout the later chapters of the book, until chapter 10, where we look in some detail at the concept of prototyping. Prototyping of software is another means of improving the quality of the software specification. But whereas formal methods improve the quality of the *description* of the requirements, prototyping improves the *understanding* of the requirements. We describe ways in which these two techniques can be combined to give a double improvement in quality.

To give specific examples of the use of a formal method, we have chosen to use the VDM (Vienna Development Method) formal specification method within this book, but the ideas which we discuss apply to other methods too.

A traditional approach to teaching Formal Methods begins by considering some discrete mathematics and then introduces the concepts of Formal Specification Techniques. Finally these ideas can be related to the software development process. We have chosen to adopt the alternative approach which is described above for the following reasons:

1. We believe that students who understand why Formal Methods are important are better motivated to learn the necessary mathematical background

2. When the reasons for its use are understood, much of the mathematics needed becomes clearer and simpler to understand and apply

3. The concept of Formal Methods needs to be more widely known and understood.

We are particularly concerned about this last point, because we feel that many people in software development who do not use formal methods need to be aware of their existence and their application. This can be illustrated by considering the construction industry as a parallel.

In the building trade, not everybody needs to be a structural engineer, but it is necessary for everybody to have at least some understanding of what a structural engineer is and how and when structural engineers can help. The advantage of this is that when a project is being undertaken which needs the help of a structural engineer, other people involved in the project will realise that one should be employed.

In software development, there have been many changes in techniques and approaches in recent years, not just in the use of Formal

Methods and Software Engineering techniques, but also in other areas. Unfortunately, not all those engaged in software development have had the opportunity to find out what the newer methods and approaches are, or how they may be helpful.

One of the aims of this book is to provide the sort of information computer programmers and software engineers need which will help them to know whether formal methods can help in their work. We hope that many more people will gain some understanding of what formal methods are, and that some will be motivated to learn more detail about how they are used.

A second aim which we have in this book, is to persuade more people to consider using formal methods. Formal Methods are seen by many people as an application of mathematics. Mathematics is not popular with many in the population, and therefore many programmers do not consider using formal methods. In fact, formal methods do apply mathematics, but they do not use areas of mathematics familar from most school courses. Therefore it is possible for people with comparatively little formal mathematical training to become competent in the mathematics needed for the application of formal methods.

We recommend that this book should be read chapter by chapter for three reasons:

1. Some of the definitions which we use may be slightly different from similar definitions used by other authors.

2. Some of the the examples which we refer to are developed in stages through the book.

3. Some mathematical techniques are developed as the book progresses.

Most of the chapters contain both worked examples and exercises. We encourage you to try all the exercises, since they are designed to help you understand key concepts and to test your understanding before you move on to the next section. Solutions to many of the exercises appear in the appendixes. These are there to help if you are stuck, but are not intended to prescribe a particular solution, since many exercises have more than one solution and any would be equally acceptable.

When you have finished this book, we hope you will not be satisfied, but will want to go further, and recommendations for further reading are included after chapter 11.

Neville J Ford
Judith M Ford
1992

Chapter 1

The software engineering background

1.1   Introduction

This chapter is about Software Engineering. In later chapters we will see how Formal Methods can play an important part in software engineering projects. We begin by considering why the introduction of software engineering marked a new start in methods for developing computer applications. We then proceed to consider the issues which are important to software engineers, and in particular we identify the features which distinguish *high quality* software. Finally, we track through the stages in the development of a new computer system in order to place into context our later discussion of specific issues and techniques.

1.2   What is the problem?

Software engineering is a term used to describe a modern approach to the writing of computer programs. In order to appreciate the significant part which software engineering has to play in the development of computer applications, it is useful to consider for a moment the way in which the software development process has changed as computers, programming techniques and the scale of computer application have changed.

When computers were first developed, they were programmed by experts using machine code. The machine code programs were extremely difficult to write, and even harder to understand or to correct. The development of assembly language and, later, high level languages for the writing of programs each played their part in allowing programs to be better thought out and more logically presented and structured.

The methods of writing and designing programs therefore followed a natural progression, from programs written in machine code and incomprehensible to all but a very select few, to programs carefully designed and presented using a high level language, which are relatively easily understood by other programmers experienced in that language.

However, despite these developments over the period from 1940 to 1980, the quality of software produced did not increase significantly in that time. We may observe how the methods used to write the programs advanced. Many books are available which describe how the languages which provide the medium for expressing the solution to the problem advanced (e.g.Ford (1990b)). But, alongside this, the vast increases in demand for computer programs meant that the benefits gained from more easily written programs were frequently used to allow more programmers to enter the computer programming profession. Thus, we saw more programmers working to produce software of mediocre quality, rather than the exisitng number of programmers taking advantage of the opportunity to work more carefully and to be more aware of quality issues.

Computers have become more widely applied and their use has become more significant. They affect so many aspects of our day to day lives that the software quality debate has become increasingly significant.

Mistakes made as a result of bugs (errors) in the computer programs may simply be expensive to put right. Or they may cause unnecessary delays. But most worryingly, in the case of computer control of manufacturing plants or medical equipment, errors can be life threatening. The cost of employing computer programmers to search for bugs and to correct them, and to adapt existing software for new uses can also be high. Indeed, some estimates suggest that as much as 80% of the total software development costs is absorbed in the correction of poorly written program code, and the maintenance of programs which are inflexibly written.

Against this background, a new approach to program design and implementation was needed, based upon the best aspects of current practice, but making a clean break with previous strategies which had allowed so much poor quality software to be developed. The concept of Software Engineering had been established.

1.3   What is software engineering?

Software engineering applies the techniques and attitudes of other areas of engineering to the software development process. When a new road bridge is planned, it is normal to employ teams of structural and civil engineers to come up with a design and to investigate in detail such matters as

- How long will it take to build?

- How much is it going to cost?

- How will this bridge fit in with other planned developments?

- Are there alternative strategies which would be cheaper, quicker or less disruptive to existing users?

From the answers to these questions, the engineers build up a detailed picture of exactly what should be done, when, how and by whom. It is only after all this detailed planning that the actual construction is allowed to begin.

Software engineering dictates that similarly thorough planning and consideration of alternatives should be undertaken before any programs are written. It identifies too impetuous a start on the actual programming as the root cause of many of the problems associated with conventional software development strategies. Software Engineering seeks to impose rigorous methodologies on the team of software engineers in order to avoid any possible problems. The careful planning and design work undertaken should ensure that the solution which is actually implemented is not just a satisfactory solution to the problem tackled, but is demonstrably better than the alternatives which have been thoroughly considered.

But it is not sufficient that specific *methodologies* are employed, the whole software development process needs to have a motive of quality control if the work of the software engineering team is to be successful.

The title and reason for this book is the introduction to the reader of **formal methods**, which is one of the tools at the disposal of the software engineer in the development of new computer systems. However, before we look in detail at this specific tool, we need to set it against the background of those other tools and methods which are also a part of the software engineer's work.

1.4   What is quality software?

The whole motivation for the software engineering process was the improvement of software quality, and we have already mentioned some of the issues involved in judging software quality. In this subsection we can draw together the issues already identified and give a more formal definition of quality. The ideas outlined here follow Sommerville (1989).

1. **The software should be maintainable.** During the lifetime of a software package, it will no doubt have to function against a changing background. Thus it will have to cope, for example, with new practices elsewhere in the company where it is used, and will have to interface with various other hardware. Maintainability relates to the ease with which the software can be adapted to suit these changing needs. This implies that one of the most important issues in maintainability is clarity, both in the programs themselves and in the supporting documentation which explains their function.

2. **The software needs to be reliable.** Reliability is obviously an important factor, but it is a wider issue than simply demanding that the program does not break down. Reliability questions need to take into account working practices as well as the actual inputs and outputs of a system. For example, a program which needs lots of data to be entered will be much more reliable if the data entry can be split up into several shorter periods rather than insisting on a single unbroken data entry session. The chances of

a hardware failure while machines are left unattended over lunch-breaks is far higher than it is at other times. Good quality software is also at pains to help the user to adopt good practices, reminding about the taking of backup copies, for example.

3. **Software should be efficient.** We want our programs to run using the minimum amount of resources. This means minimising the use of staff and processor time and of memory and disk space. However, it is not always best to optimise fully the resource use, since to do so may make the program more difficult to understand or maintain, and so a balance must be sought between, on the one hand, full optimisation, and on the other, easy maintainability.

4. **The software should offer an appropriate user interface.** It is always important to remember the final end-user of any software package, and to remember that problems with the user interface are the most common cause of complaints and of user errors. The user should be helped to avoid mistakes and be given sensible opportunities to make corrections. On the other hand, some packages become unwieldy in use because they offer too many opportunities to correct errors. Many users complain constantly of the programs which ask them repeatedly *are you sure?*

The work which we shall cover in the present book concerns mainly the first two issues listed here. For software to be easily maintainable it is important that we have a very clear understanding of its present specification, the proposed new specification and of the precise way in which it is designed to meet these. Reliability is also dependent on a similarly clear understanding of the systems design and specification.

1.5 The systems development process

If we consider, for a while, the processes involved in the design and introduction of a new computer system, then we will have a clearer view of the impact of these quality issues, and we shall also be able to focus on those stages in the process which are particularly significant to us and where formal methods can most advantageously be applied. The discussion here merges those aspects of systems development which are traditionally considered to be the province of the systems analyst with those which are generally termed software engineering. The processes are illustrated in figure 1.1.

The initial motivation for changing computer systems comes from a company's management. Usually triggered by some business need, such as the need to expand, to improve cash flow, to cut down on customer complaints or to cut staff, the first problem is to determine whether or not there is any possibility of a successful and economical solution to the perceived problem

The initial investigation, carried out by a trained team of analysts recommends on whether or not to carry out a further feasibility study, which provides a fairly detailed account of the proposed systems development. At this stage, the important issues are to decide just what should be the terms of reference for the development of the new system, and to make recommendations on the proposed budget for the development. The idea, at least in theory, is that the feasibility study should provide an opportunity to avoid spending lots of money on developing a new system which either does not perform satisfactorily, or is no better than the existing system, or whose cost is unacceptably high.

A more detailed study follows the feasibility report. In this report, much more information is gathered about the ways in which jobs are completed at present, and details are deduced about just what are the requirements of the system. Modern methods using *structured techniques* come into play at this stage of the investigation.

Models of the system can be established, and some experts devise different models to represent different ways of looking at the system. For example, we might construct a model which illustrates the way in which data moves around the existing system. Where does it go, who stores it, and so on. Or we might look at the ways in which different documents move around the system. Why, for example, do we need to have three copies of a particular form- who needs each one, and why? Then we might consider the ways in which different *entities* in the system relate to one another. How does the sales desk, the accounts department and the warehouse inter-relate in the system?

The advantage of system modelling from these different perspectives is that it helps to give the investigating team a clear idea of exactly what

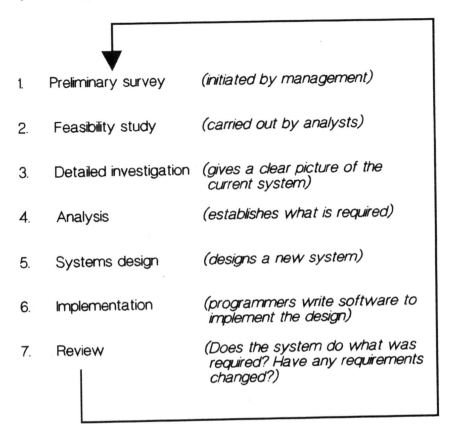

1. Preliminary survey   *(initiated by management)*

2. Feasibility study   *(carried out by analysts)*

3. Detailed investigation   *(gives a clear picture of the current system)*

4. Analysis   *(establishes what is required)*

5. Systems design   *(designs a new system)*

6. Implementation   *(programmers write software to implement the design)*

7. Review   *(Does the system do what was required? Have any requirements changed?)*

Figure 1.1 The systems life-cycle

happens within the existing system which they are investigating. These ideas go to make up a clear statement of the *physical* characteristics of the existing system. The aim in designing a new system is to produce a new physical design which describes the way in which the new system will operate.

However it is not always easy to move from one physical design directly to another. People have preconceptions about the ways in which particular things must be done, because they can see how these things are done at the moment. It may therefore be helpful (and usually is) to construct a *logical* design for the system. This attempts to remove all the methods which are identified on the current physical model, and concentrates instead on what exactly is being done. The logical design therefore gives a clear *lowest common denominator* view of the existing system's performance. This is the stage at which the design of the new system is best begun.

The current logical system is adapted, taking into account the aspirations for the new system and any complaints about the old system, to give a proposed logical model. It is this proposed logical model which is finally developed into a proposed physical model which describes the ways in which the new system will work. The result of all this analysis and design based upon the existing system will be termed the *Requirements Definition* document. It is with the requirements definition document that Software Engineers are initially concerned from a traditional standpoint.

The requirements definition makes a clear general statement about the objectives of the new system. The document identifies the *functional requirements* which list the things which the system needs to do, alongside the *non-functional requirements* which give details of the way in which the system must behave. Thus, in a payroll system, the fact that the system must produce payslips is a functional requirement. The fact that this must happen on the third Thursday in each month is a non-functional requirement.

Alongside these lists of functional and non-functional requirements will be other documentation from earlier stages in the software development process, including diagrams of system models which have been constructed, and other relevant information about operating procedures.

The software engineer works on this information to produce the Software Specification document. This document identifies the various subsystems which will exist within the completed software package and makes clear statements about the ways in which data is to be collected, stored and processed. The role of the software engineer in the construction of suitable data structures for the application is often seen as secondary to the role of developing algorithms, but more recently the importance of data analysis has been recognised. This is the stage at which a clear statement is being made about exactly what the programs are going to do. It must be made clearly and unambiguously and be in a form which is readily understood by other members of the development team. Various different approaches to this specification of requirements have been tried, and we will discuss these in later chapters.

The requirements definition and software specification documents are held alongside all further developments of the computer system, because they contain the formal description of what each component of the system will do. It forms the basis for testing whether the programs perform to specification, and for any future modifications of the system. This reinforces the desire to have the requirements definition and systems specification documents as well presented as possible.

A key issue here, and one not always recognised in software development, is the way in which intentions change during the software development process. So although the original software specification might make it very clear that modules within the development of a program should inter-relate in a particular way, it might become clear while working at a later stage that the inter-relationships should be varied to take into account a new improved understanding of the problem. But unfortunately, while this *iterative* approach to software development is to be applauded, developers frequently make the changes at the later stage autonomously, and fail to make the corresponding changes to the requirements definition and software specification.

A document as important within the development process as the software specification, needs to be carefully checked, both for consistency with itself, and for whether or not it conveys the required specification accurately. The process of requirements validating and of the development of prototype systems may assist in this checking process.

Once the software specification document is accepted,

implementation may begin. Various methods of program design and development are in use, and these are beyond the scope of this book. Sommerville (1989) gives a clear description of some of the most important strategies in widespread use.

As soon as the programs are complete, even in embrionic form, they must be tested and their performance validated. The software specification document comes back into use at this stage, since it should, ideally, define clearly the ways in which the programs and the individual modules should behave. Thus the testing should, at least in theory, be predetermined by the software specification.

In practice, these documents do not always give a clear, complete and unambiguous statement of the needs of a system. This means that programmers are left unclear about whether their testing is adequate (or in the worst cases, what the outcome of their tests should be). This is a major cause for concern in the software quality debate, and as such, is one of the areas which the use of formal methods discussed later seeks to address.

1.6   Alternative strategies

The strategy for the design of a computerised system which we have described here is based upon a variation of the traditional *systems life cycle* described in conventional systems analysis textbooks. The approach is to begin with the users and managers of the present system, identify strengths and weaknesses and then to move onto an understanding of how a new replacement system should behave. This approach has been developed in the ways described above to provide a more rigorous approach to systems development, but still within the same broad framework, and this is the way in which software engineering techniques have been introduced in systems within the author's experience.

However, it is important to recognise that there are some experts in the area who consider the traditional systems life cycle approach to be so fundamentally flawed that it should be rejected out of hand. These computer scientists argue for a completely new approach which does not draw from the systems life cycle at all. Some people would apply the techniques of the Vienna Development Method, discussed later in this book, without reference to the traditional life-cycle approach, and we shall discuss this strategy in more detail when we look at prototyping of software.

There are others who maintain that techniques introduced at various stages of the system design should be employed in different ways. Thus, there are those who adopt an approach to systems development based upon a rigid approach which follows the methods of SSADM, an approach approved by the UK Government for all public sector developments. Others, while espousing the techniques of one methodology, argue that no single methodology should be applied rigidly, because to do this restricts creativity to the terms of reference of the method. On the other hand, ad hoc variations in a clearly defined method may lead to ambiguity and misunderstanding, so there are arguments both ways.

One particular problem highlighted by Gane (1990) concerns methods which insist on deriving the proposed logical model from the current model. The problem is that while this approach brings great benefits in most cases, there is a tendency to *rebuild in* the very restrictions on performance from the old system which the new system is designed to remove. Therefore the Gane/Sarson method makes a clear distinction between other methods which might force reliance on a current physical model, and their method which presents two alternative strategies for system development: the one based upon a current physical → current logical → proposed logical → proposed physical series, the other based upon rejecting the current implementation altogether and constructing a current logical/physical model from scratch. (Figure 1.2).

1.7   Questions for discussion

1. Which do you consider likely to be quicker, designing a system using software engineering techniques, or applying more traditional methods?

2. What pressures on companies might result in them choosing to produce software of low quality?

3. How does the work of software engineers affect the job of systems analysts?

4. Under what circumstances might it be inappropriate to start system modelling from the current physical system model?

Method 1

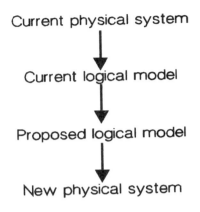

Method 2.

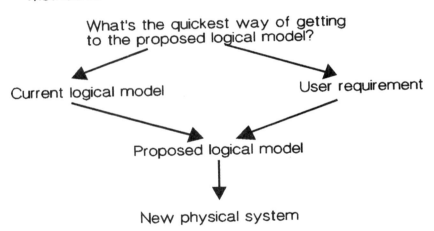

Figure 1.2 Two alternative strategies for system development

Chapter 2

Software Specification and Verification

2.1 Introduction

In the previous chapter, the methods of software engineering have been highlighted and identified as providing appropriate tools for the development of high quality software. We have seen that high quality software is well designed and carefully implemented.

This chapter focuses on a crucial stage in the software engineering process: the software specification document. Software specification forms the basis for much of the software engineer's work and therefore it is important that the document is prepared rigorously and accurately. It is in the preparation of and uses of this *software specification document* that the work of the remainder of this book will focus.

2.2 The Software Specification document

Unfortunately, the titles given to the documents produced at the various stages of a software engineering project are not fixed. Different software engineers produce documents at different stages in the process, and give the documents produced a variety of names. Thus, it is likely that other books on the subject will use different titles for the documents from the ones which we shall describe. It is therefore helpful to begin by thinking about the stages in the software development and to make clear exactly the stage which we are assuming that we have reached.

2.2.1   The work of the systems analyst

The systems analyst begins the project by conducting interviews. The interviews are used to determine, first, whether there is a project which is worth undertaking; second, how much the project is likely to cost; and third, the precise terms of reference for the subsequent development work.

The first report produced by the systems analyst is generally called the **feasibility study**. This recommends whether there is any particular project which should be undertaken, and considers the likely costs and benefits of the project.

The second report produced by the systems analyst is sometimes known as the **requirements specification**. This report describes in some detail what exactly the newly defined system should accomplish. The systems analyst's requirements specification is the product of a series of interviews, possibly the responses to questionnaires, and observations of existing systems and practices.

In a software development project undertaken by software engineers, we shall find it helpful to assume that work equivalent to these two reports have already been completed before the software engineers begin their work. We shall therefore be in a position to assume that the systems analyst has already completed the reports and that they are readily available to the software engineers for reference. (Figure (2.1).)

The software engineers now need to begin to construct the document which we shall refer to as the software specification. (Note the distinction which we are making between the *software specification* document, which we think of as an engineer's document and the *requirements specification* which we shall think of, for the time being as a systems analyst's document.

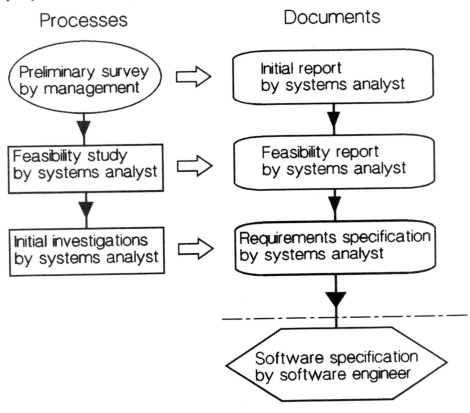

Figure 2.1 The systems analyst carries out the initial investigations before the software engineer starts work

2.2.2   The contents of the Software Specification document

The software specification document consists of two parts. In the first part, the software engineers put together a definition of exactly what is the task which is to be completed. We shall call this sub-document the **requirements definition** document. The material which goes into the requirements definition document can often be based very closely upon the work which is completed by the systems analyst in the earlier requirements specification document, and the document may, as has been stated, take a variety of forms. We shall consider (for convenience) a form of requirements definition document which seems to us both simple and fairly complete. It contains

- Introduction: an introduction to the organisation, indicating the general area of the project and its scope and size.

- System model: it can be convenient to represent a system by means of a model. Systems models are becoming a natural tool for systems analysts. The model is usually represented as a diagram which shows inter-relationships of different parts of the system. These representations can be particularly helpful in seeing inter-relationships between existing areas and areas which are involved in new developments. They can also help the concurrent development of more than one part of a system by different teams of software engineers. Different approaches to system modelling adopt different conventions; any one or all of them may be appropriate in a particular situation. System models may therefore focus on the movement of data, and/or on the movement of documents, and/or on the relationships of different elements (entities) of the system, and/or on the life history of a particular task or data item. There are corresponding diagrammatic representations for each of these. The data flow diagram is popular and is illustrated (figure 2.2). For more details of how data flow diagrams are constructed and for details of othe suitable diagrams, we refer the reader to Cutts (1987).

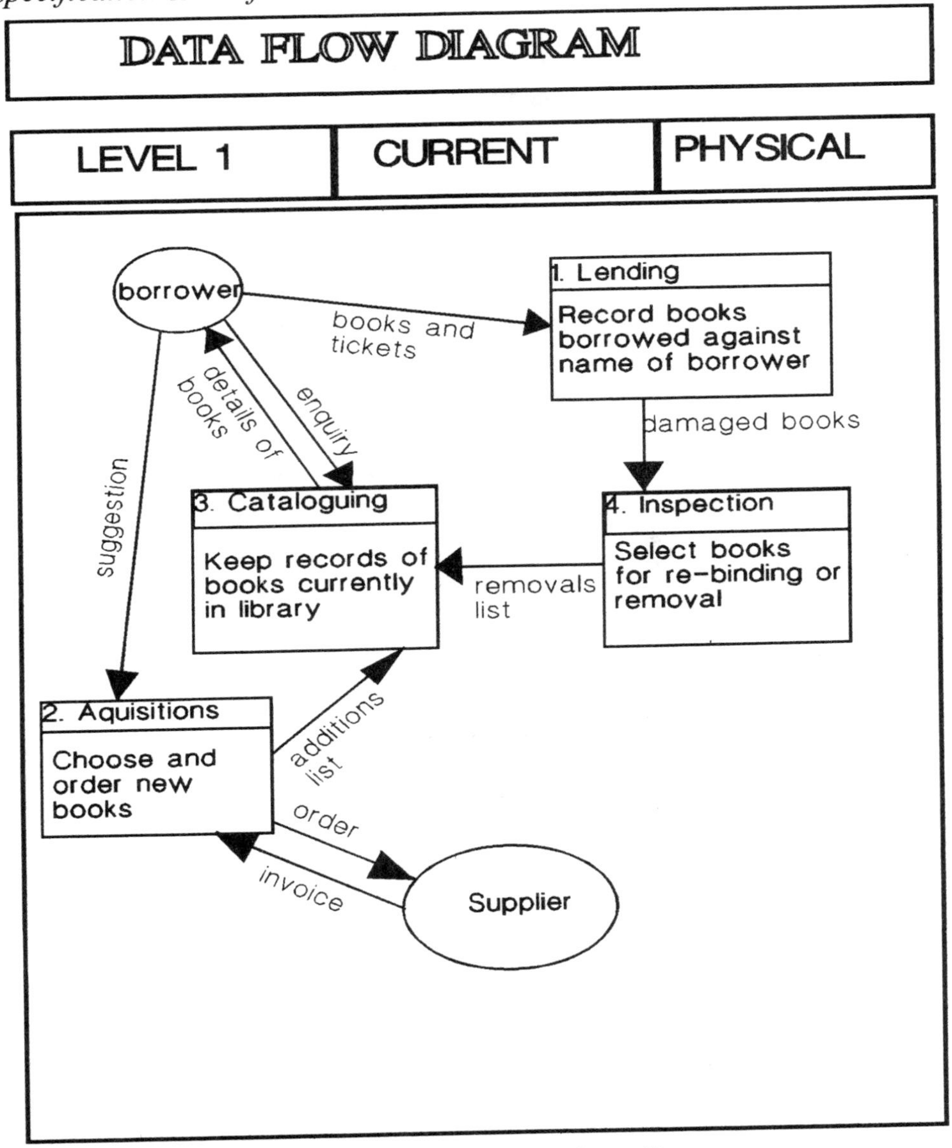

Figure 2.2 A typical data flow diagram

- Functional requirements: one of the principal purposes in installing a new system is in order to do something! This may be encapsulated by a simple single statement, such as 'Computerise the payroll' or may be something more complex, such as 'find a more efficient way of providing stock information so that more orders are fulfilled within 24 hours of their receipt'. It is therefore appropriate at this stage to try to make a clear statement of exactly what it is that a new system is aiming to do. These requirements are known as the **functional requirements**. Functional requirements are distinct from the various qualitative requirements of *how* the system should perform, which are listed later as the **non-functional requirements**. The functional requirements for a system are presented as a numbered list of functions (operations) which the system should undertake.

For example, for a system to control the borrowing of books from a public library, we might have the following functional requirements:

F1 A list of borrowers is to be maintained

F2 A catalogue of books is to be held

F3 Records are to be kept of borrowers and which books they have

F4 Reminders should be sent to borrowers with overdue books

F5 Fines should be calculated

Making a list of functional requirements is a very useful exercise, because it forces the software developer to consider in detail what are the requirements of the system. Similarly, it helps the software engineer not to be constrained by preconceived notions of how the various parts of the system are to function. It is all too common for constraints on a system to be imposed unwittingly simply because of the desire to reproduce a property of an existing system, when that property is no longer really required. Forcing the production of a list of these functional requirements therefore has the effect of highlighting just what is, and what is not, to be included in the completed system.

These lists of functional requirements are then refined gradually as the development process continues. For example, the requirement which we have identified here as F1 could be refined in the following way:

F1 A list of borrowers is to be maintained

F1.1 New borrowers can be added to the list

F1.2 Details of borrowers can be changed when they marry, move house or change category

F1.3 Borrowers can be deleted from the list

This provides an early illustration of the *dynamic* nature of the documents which we are producing. They are not intended simply to provide a record that particular tasks have been completed, but they are an intrinsic part of the software development process. The requirements definition document which is current at the end of a project should have many changes incorporated in it so that it reflects the state of understanding of the project at the end of the project and not simply the state of understanding at the beginning when the initial work on the project began. This *dynamic approach to documentation* is one of the features which is essential for the production of high quality software.

A second feature of software engineering which is illustrated here, and which we shall refer to often in this work, is the fact that writing functional requirements forces us to think anew about features of a system which we previously believed that we understood fully. It is precisely this thinking again about operations and procedures in a new light which gives some of the power to the formal methods which we meet later in this book.

- Hardware: Typically the hardware requirements for a system will be constrained either by the budget imposed by the systems analysts during the feasibility study, or by the desire to utilise existing facilities. Therefore the requirements definition document lists hardware available as a constraint on the development process.

- Database requirements: All data processing systems exist to process data, and the majority of computer applications currently developed are data processing applications. It is natural therefore to give some thought to the actual data which will need to be stored. In a typical project, at this stage it is important to identify the contents of the data record which will need to be stored about each entity which forms a part of the system under development and to determine at a later stage in the software engineering process just how the data should be stored and processed.

- Non-functional requirements: Non functional requirements describe qualities of a system rather than capabilities. For example a non-functional requirement of a system might be that it should produce the payslips on Thursdays, or that it should be able to find any customer's address in less than 20 seconds. Non-functional requirements are crucially important to the software engineer because they are often thought about too late to incorporate in the software, and yet it is precisely the qualities which are non-functional which colour individual people's opinions of the *quality* of the software.

- Maintenance information: Details are listed about the likely life of the system which is to be developed and the costs which have been allocated to cover future changes and upgrades. It is appropriate that the software engineers should record

    1. those foreseeable changes to the program which are to be incorporated from the start
    2. also those foreseeable changes for which provision should be made for future add-ons.

It is also appropriate that, for example, the desire to convert all the programs to new and incompatible hardware in the near future should be taken into account here.

- Glossary and index.

This completes the requirements definition document, which forms the basis of the agreement between software engineer and client. The document is prepared by the software engineer in consultation with the systems analyst and then agreed with the client. Various models for the production of the document have been proposed. Some people favour the systems analyst producing the requirements definition document as we have described it here, instead of producing the requirements specification document more usually produced by the analyst. This approach would save time and money since only one document is produced, rather than two. On the other hand, it can be argued that the work of the software engineer in

- understanding the systems analyst's document

- converting the information it contains into an alternative form

- arguing details with the systems analyst

keeps the quality of the work of both professionals involved as high as possible. The importance of ironing out misunderstandings at this early stage and the consequent savings in time later in the project can then be used to justify the apparent extra cost.

The second part of the software specification document is a more technical document, which is produced by the software engineers working from the requirements definition document. Unfortunately, to add to the confusion about document titles, this sub-document is frequently called the requirements specification document. This ambiguity is highlighted and explained by figure 2.3.

The aim of the requirements specification part of the software specification document is to provide for the software engineer a formal and rigorous description of the software which is to be developed. The idea is that, by making sure that the requirements of the system are clearly enough specified at this stage, it will be clearer whether the actual program which is the final outcome of the project satisfies its requirements.

Historically, software engineers and programmers have been forced to use **informal methods** to specify their software. These informal methods are described in the next chapter, and we will see that they leave something to be desired when judged as a means to providing a clear and unambiguous description. On the other hand, formal methods which are introduced in chapter 4, are not easy to get started with, and

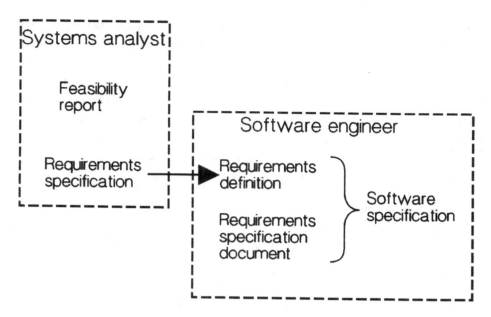

Figure 2.3 Both the systems analyst and the software engineer produce documents known as the *requirements specification*. It is important not to confuse the two.

are thought by many to be impossibly complicated to use. We hope to convince the reader that the principles involved are straightforward and worthwhile, even if some of the arguments may seem unnecessarily complex and abstract at first.

For the present, we concern ourselves with the further questions of judging quality software, since this is intertwined with the matter of software specification.

2.3   Quality software specification

Since we have identified the software specification document as crucial in the development of High Quality Software, it is appropriate to ask *What features should a good software specification display?*

The software specification describes the problem which is to be solved and makes statements about what the solution of the problem should be like. It is therefore clearly essential that the document is

- Clear and unambiguous

- Accurate

- Complete

We shall see in later chapters how different methods of describing the software specification possess different properties which relate to these three desirable characteristics. There is also an additional property of software specifications which is desirable but which is less immediately obvious. We desire that a specification should be *implementation independent*. In other words, the software specification is required to focus carefully upon *what the software has to do* but should not take into account how the software is to be written. We shall spend some time later in this book discussing this issue in more detail from a variety of viewpoints. For the present, it is sufficient to identify implementation independence of the specification as an important issue. This is because we need to be clear when we make statements about what the software needs to do that we are making no compromises. Compromises in specification can conceal important requirements and lead to disatisfaction for the client.

To ensure that the specification written is complete and accurate, we need to verify and validate the requirements. This is the subject of the next section.

2.4   Validation and Verification of Requirements and Software

After specifying clearly in the software specification document exactly what the objectives of the software development will be, there are two types of testing of the software specification which may be undertaken, these are

- Requirements validation

- Software verification.

The two types of checking are completely different, and must be undertaken at very different stages.

2.4.1   Requirements validation

In requirements validation, we are considering the design specification which we are working to, and we are asking the question, 'will software produced to meet the given specification genuinely meet our needs?'

The specification document is important here, because it is only when the software has been clearly and rigorously specified that we can be in a position to answer this question. Requirements validation is the counterpart of the market research which would be undertaken by a manufacturer of motor cars who wanted to ensure that a new design really met the desires and needs of the target group of customers. Requirements validation is described by some authors as answering the question 'are we making the right product?'

2.4.2   Software verification

Having decided on the right product, it then becomes very important to be sure that it is well made. The issue of software verification is concerned with checking that the programs which are written do indeed match with the specification which has been developed. It is therefore crucial that the specification is:

- clear

- unambiguous

- complete.

Software verification is described by some authors as answering the question 'are we making the product right?'

2.4.3   Approaches to requirements validation

Obviously requirements validation can be undertaken by the systems analyst as an on-going part of the systems analysis process. At each stage of the process, interim reports of the findings can be made and shown to management and others who have been interviewed for cross-checking to ensure that the requirements have been correctly and completely recorded. However it is often the case that changes to the requirements are made at a very late stage in the software development process because problems with the original specification have been missed by all concerned.

It is difficult to provide any reliable method of avoiding these last-minute problems being identified, but there are two particular approaches which can be helpful:

Experienced systems analysts can bring their previous project experience to bear upon the present problem. It can be the case that the same omissions in the specification will have been made in previous projects. Therefore a comparison of the specification of the current problem with similar project specifications made previously can be helpful in ironing out problems.

Accepting that many users find it very difficult to identify problems with a specification expressed on paper and only really appreciate its shortcomings when faced with a real working system, the aim of producing a very early prototype system is appropriate. We shall discuss several methods of working to a rapid prototye which can be used in testing the design. This discussion appears in chapter 10.

2.4.4   Approaches to software verification

As we have described, software verification means checking that the software which has been written provides a faithful implementation of the specification. This is an issue which is fundamental to much of the contents of this book, because the whole issue of the use of a *formal method* for specifying a computer system only really becomes worthwhile when it leads to the production of higher quality software which must therefore be well implemented. We shall be discussing features of implementations which *realise* their objectives and therefore are described as *realisations* of the given specification.

Traditionally, software verification has been undertaken by means of **testing**. In other words, when a program has been written, it is tested in various ways in order to ensure that the program performs in the way it should.

For most complex programs, a system of testing known as *bottom-up testing* is employed. Here the program is developed in a *modular* manner, by writing sections of the program to undertake specific tasks and then joining the modules together to form larger subsections of the program, before finally producing the completed program (figure 2.4). Bottom-up testing adopts the attitude that it is appropriate to test that the individual procedures are correct, then to test each sub-program before finally testing the completed program. Therefore there is significant work involved in determining, first, what data should be used in order to test each module, and second, in writing small programs which can be used to test each module.

Selecting test data is a highly complex operation, because it is important that the data selected should test the programs thoroughly and exhaustively. In other words, the test data must be chosen so that every possible route through the program is tested. If the program behaves differently for men and for women, then it must be tested with men and with women. If it behaves differerently for the over 30s from the under 30s then it must be tested for men over 30, men under 30, women over 30 and women under 30. It needs to be tested for typical data and with exceptional data to ensure that the necessary procedures which deal with exceptional situations function correctly. It may be observed that the problem of testing programs adequately is not easy.

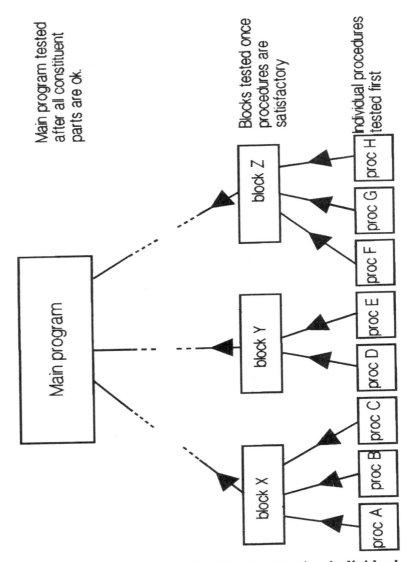

Figure 2.4 Bottom-up testing involves testing individual procedures first, then blocks of ready-tested procedures, and so on.

Typically, therefore, programs are inadequately tested. Adequate exhaustive testing takes too long, and is, in any case, subject to mistakes being made by the tester who omits to consider a particular test case. Therefore alternatives to testing have been sought.

One alternative to testing is the use of a **proof of conformance** to the specification based upon the formal definition of the software specification, expressed using a formal language. In chapter 4, we shall see how this can be accomplished for a simple example. Unfortunately the quantity of work involved in proving equivalence by hand in this way can be prohibitive for many applications.

Other alternative methods are also proposed for the production of reliable software. One which is appealing is the use of previously tested code. Sometimes, even frequently, it is apparent that a particular part of a program is actually equivalent to part of another program which has already been written. Therefore if there is already in existence a suitable procedure which has been fully tested and conforms with the new specification, then the use of the existing procedure is highly efficient and reliable.

Therefore it can be appropriate to build up libraries of procedures which perform common operations and which are likely to be applicable elsewhere. The cost and effort involved in providing proofs of satisfiability in these cases is then more likely to be justified, since, as we shall see later, the proof of satisfiability admits no possible error to be found in the future. Some libraries of existing procedures are available commercially, and they generally seem to be of high quality although details of the methods used to confirm that they satisfy their specifications is only rarely given.

2.5   Exercises

1. For a computer system which operates your bank's accounts, write a list of

   - Functional requirements
   - Non-functional requirements

2. Why is it important that software is correctly specified?

3. Look critically at some computer programs which you have written.

   - Have you specified the requirements clearly before you started?
   - Could the programs be verified against the specification? (In answering this question, you may reach a conclusion either on the quality of the specification, or on the quality of your programming!)

4. Can you think of any reasons why the use of previously tested program code might compromise the quality of a specification?

Chapter 3

Informal Methods

3.1   Introduction

In this chapter, we shall develop our discussion of the software specification from chapter 2. In particular, we shall consider the Requirements Definition and Requirements Specification documents. We have discussed already what these documents should contain, in terms of the information which will need to be presented, but this leaves open the crucial question of how the information is to be presented. In the current chapter, we shall discuss various approaches to the presentation of this, and these ideas will be evaluated and developed in later chapters.

3.2   Key components of the Requirements Definition

We identified in the previous chapter the fundamental distinction between the *requirements definition* and the *requirements specification*, and we chose to follow the distinction between these two terms used by Sommerville (1989).

It is the intention of the **requirements definition** to provide information on the objectives of the new system development in a form which is *easily accessible to the management of the employing company*. The requirements definition thus forms the basis of the understanding between the systems analysts and software engineers and the employing company, and in order to satisfy this objective, the document must be written in an easily understood way.

On the other hand, the **requirements specification** is a much more technical document which forms the basis for communication between the systems analysts, the software engineers and other project personnel. The universal understanding of the language and technical terminology used in this document therefore takes second place to the importance of a clear and unambiguous document. This is because the users of this latter document are technically competent specialists who may be expected to become familiar with whatever method of expressing ideas might be chosen for a project.

So far as the requirements definition is concerned, we shall be concerned principally with the problem of expressing lists of functional and non-functional requirements for the proposed system. The natural language to use in this respect is English, which should be clearly understood by both the managers of the organisation employing the software developers and by the computer specialists themselves.

3.3   Case study

In order to gain a clearer view of the requirements definition document, we shall think about the requirements of a library which is considering installing a new computerised book issuing system, and we shall consider the functional and non-functional requirements of such a system:

1. Functional requirements

    (a) A list of books shall be maintained

    (b) A list of borrowers' names and addresses shall be maintained

    (c) A record of books borrowed by each borrower shall be kept

    (d) Fines shall be calculated for overdue books

    (e) Reminders shall be printed for overdue books

    (f) Special book requests and orders shall be dealt with

(g) A catalogue and information service shall be available to users who need to search for a book

(h) Summary information about book usage and popularity shall be available

2. Non-functional requirements

(a) The system shall be easy to use

(b) Training requirements for operators should be minimised

(c) The system should be fast enough to avoid queues

(d) The system should be reliable

(e) Library users as well as staff should be able to use parts of the system directly

3.3.1   Exercise

Look at the list of functional and non-functional requirements given here and consider your own experience of public library services. Make a list of any additional requirements you would want to add to the lists, dividing your requirements between functional and non-functional.

We are concerned in this chapter with ways of expressing requirements, and it is therefore appropriate to look at the list of requirements which we have given here. One thing to notice immediately, is that such a list is never complete, nor is it usually wholly satisfactory. We are generally faced with a choice between the following possibilities:

- Giving a list of requirements which is sufficiently general to be all-embracing, but so imprecise as to be almost useless

- We can give a fully itemised list which makes clear the details of some of the activities, but leaves the way open for omissions to be criticised.

The following alternative lists give some indication of the first extreme.

1. Functional requirements

    (a) A list of books shall be maintained

    (b) A list of borrowers' names and addresses shall be maintained

    (c) All normal library activities shall be catered for

2. Non-functional requirements

    (a) The system shall be efficient and easy to use

The advantage of this list is that it can be argued that it is all-embracing. However, the amount of additional information which it contains, over and above a title to the project, such as 'Library Computerisation', is minimal.

One way in which this problem may be overcome is to identify the functional and non-functional requirements under broad headings and then to subdivide (or, *refine*) the original list of broad requirements to give a more detailed list, but one which still reflects the overview. For the present example, this might have the following appearance:

1. Functional requirements

    (a) A list of books shall be maintained

    (b) A list of borrowers' names and addresses shall be maintained

    (c) All normal library activities shall be catered for

        i. A record of books borrowed by each borrower shall be kept

        ii. Fines shall be calculated for overdue books

        iii. Reminders shall be printed for overdue books

        iv. Special book requests and orders shall be dealt with

        v. A catalogue and information service shall be available to users who need to search for a book

        vi. Summary information about book usage and popularity shall be available

2. Non-functional requirements

(a) The system shall be efficient and easy to use

    i. The system shall be easy to use

    ii. Training requirements for operators should be minimised

    iii. The system should be fast enough to avoid queues

    iv. The system should be reliable

    v. Library users as well as staff should be able to use parts of the system directly

The advantages of expressing the requirements in this way are clear:

- The simple list of overall requirements is retained

- The list may be extended in detail gradually as understanding of the requirements develops

- The criticism that more detail can mean that some important features are omitted is avoided since the broadly-based requirements are retained

3.3.2 Exercise

The functional requirements for a stock control system for a warehouse are listed below. Using the refinement techniques discussed here, rewrite an extended list of functional requirements which gives more detail of the tasks which will need to be undertaken by the system. After you have completed your consideration of functional requirements, try to think of an appropriate list of non-functional requirements.

Functional requirements

1. A list of items held and their stock level shall be kept

2. A list of orders waiting to be despatched shall be kept

3. A list of orders of new stock awaited shall be kept

4. Orders shall be processed

5. Invoices shall be processed

6. Accounts shall be maintained

In the discussion so far, we have been concerned with items which can only sensibly be described in English (or, to be technical, 'in a *natural language'*). Nevertheless, we have identified an approach which will be important within many of our subsequent discussions: the method of *refinement* of a list of overall requirements into a more detailed list of specific requirements.

3.4   Key components of the Requirements Specification

As we identified at the beginning of the chapter, the requirements specification document is not constrained by the need to be intelligible to the non-technical reader in the way that the requirements definition was. We are, therefore, free to consider various ways of expressing our ideas, including the use of technical terminology, or of specialised notations and methods.

The aim at this stage in the development of a new system is to present material which describes the proposed system in terms of what functions it will perform (the 'functional view') and the data which it must store (the 'data view').

One important objective is that we try to retain an *implementation free* approach for as long as is feasible. In other words, we shall try to explore ways of expressing just what the system is going to do without pre-supposing just how it will go about doing this!

In order to get some clearer understanding of what is contained within the requirements specification document, we shall consider the library system case study in some detail. For simplicity, we will subdivide our discussion between the functional view of the system and the data view. In this work, we consider the data view first:

3.4.1   The data view of the system

The discussion of data within a system involves the determination of an appropriate data structure or data structures for the storage and processing of the information which the system requires. The choice of appropriate data structures is in itself quite a complex activity. It involves, among other things:

- Considering the form of the data which is to be stored

- Considering the different ways in which the data is to be processed

- Considering the speed requirements of the proposed system

- Taking into account any constraints imposed by hardware and software

When we look at this list of constraints, we can immediately see that there is a conflict here between our previous statement, that we need to try to make our specification document as implementation independent as is possible, and the requirement listed here that we shall take into account constraints imposed by hardware and software, which are clearly dependent upon decisions about implementation which will be made subsequently. This is just one of the conflicts faced by the software engineer in this area. The only satisfactory way to overcome the problem this imposes is to make two observations:

- The software specification document is a document which should be revised as the implementation of the project continues. In other words, we should not expect to be in a position to complete a finally complete and immutable version of the software specification document at this stage. Rather it is important that we produce a statement at this point which makes as many points as possible clear, so that the need for changes as systems development advances are kept to a minimum.

- The requirements specification should attempt at this stage to take account of any obvious constraints which will arise regardless of the implementation method which is later selected, but not impose too many arbitrary constraints which might prove unnecessarily restrictive.

The selection of appropriate data structures for the storage of data ready for subsequent processing is a complex task. One of the weaknesses of computer software developed is often a direct result of an inappropriate choice of fundamental data structure for the program. Therefore, in this work, alongside many other books in the broad area of software engineering, we have chosen to discuss the choice of data structures before the specification of functions and procedures, in an attempt to emphasise the key importance of this task.

There are a number of standard data structures which might be used, and from within this list there is usually either one appropriate to our needs, or one of the standard ones may be relatively easily adapted to suit a particular situation. The following list is not exhaustive, but covers a some of the simplest and most common data structures:

- The stack

- The queue

- The priority queue

- The unordered list

- The ordered list

- The tree.

3.4.2   What is a data structure?

We have here identified a collection of items which we have termed data structures. But what, exactly, is a data structure?

In order to answer this question, we shall return to our consideration of the library computerisation example from earlier. Now we know from the functional requirements of the system under development, that we shall need to store details of all the books held by the library. We have a clear idea from experience what sort of information we will be storing:

- Author

- Title

- Publisher

- Classification number in the library

- Acquisition number

- Price paid by the library

We also know from the functional requirements listed, and from our experience, that the following operations will be needed, all of which depend in some way upon the way in which the data on books held by the library may be processed:

- Find the class number from the title or author

- Find out whether the book required is on loan to another borrower

- Add extra books to the catalogue when they are purchased

- Remove lost or damaged books from the catalogue

These two lists begin to give us a clearer understanding of what we shall need to have when we set up the data structure for storing the catalogue of books in the library: we have details of the information which will need to be stored, and we have details of the processing requirements for that information.

We will therefore define an **abstract data structure** in precisely this way. We say that an abstract data structure consists of an account of the data which is to be stored, together with a list of the procedures which will be used to manipulate the data.

We might then ask: Why do we call this an *abstract* data structure, rather than just a data structure? The answer to this lies in the implementation. When we define an abstract data structure, we are making clear what it is that we need to do. On the other hand, we shall implement these requirements later, and at that stage we will have to determine just how the data is to be stored within the system, and just how the procedures are going to be written so that they will satisfy their specification. It is during the implementation phase that the abstract data structures take on their concrete form.

The data structures which we listed earlier, The stack, the queue, the priority queue, the unordered list, the ordered list, and the tree form a collection of *abstract data structures* because they have not yet been implemented, nor indeed has their method of implementation been predetermined. We may best think of these as *template* data structures which will help us to identify familiar processing requirements within real life examples. The advantage of this is that there has been considerable research and development work already completed on these standard structures. We can find publications which make a clear statement of the needs of the various different processes for each such data structure. We can even find works which give simple procedural implementations in appropriate languages for the most common abstract data structures. (See for example Schneider and Bruell (1991)).

The existence of these standard reference books on abstract data structures is a great asset, because the problem of choosing a suitable data structure is as nothing compared to the problem of specifying *clearly and unambiguously* the processing requirements of the system as they relate to the data structure. In order to illustrate this, we will think again about the library case study.

3.5   Case study, continued

As we identified earlier, the requirements of the book cataloguing system within the library dictated the need to hold the following information on the computer system:

Author, Title, Publisher, Classification number in the library, Acquisition number, Price paid by the library

We also identified the following processing requirements:

- Find the class number from the title or author

- Find out whether the book required is on loan to another borrower

- Add extra books to the catalogue when they are purchased

- Remove lost or damaged books from the catalogue

When we look at this list of requirements, we have an immediate understanding of what is intended— or at least we think we do! In order to
think about methods of implementation, however, we need to do some
more work, and in particular, we shall need to *refine* our processing
requirements so that they become more closely mirrored in the sorts
of operations which we shall be able to implement in an appropriate
programming system.

There is an unfortunate, but unavoidable, fact that according to the
software engineer's experiences, prejudices and approaches to software
developement, it is exceedingly difficult to keep strictly to the requirement that all the following discussions should be implementation free.
This is because it is inevitable that an engineer, knowing how a particular structure has been implemented in previous projects will tend to
think in terms of the way in which it should be implemented this time,
rather than to work completely *blind*. This has some advantages as
well as the disadvantage of presupposing a particular implementation.
A software engineer who has completed a similar project previously
may well work more quickly (by avoiding false starts) and more accurately (by applying previous experiences). The only real method to
employ to overcome these prejudices is the realisation by all members
of the team that they might be bringing previous experiences to bear
on their judgement. The recognition that this could restrict their creativity is usually sufficient to ensure that alternative approaches are at
least considered.

We will now need to consider in some detail what each of these
processing requirements means in practice:

1. Find the class number from the title or author

   This process involves looking at the collection of records and comparing each one with the required title or author. When a match
   is found, the information is to be displayed on the screen.

2. Find out whether the book required is on loan to another borrower

   Having identified the book required, this process needs to compare
   the details of the book required with the details of current loans
   (however that might have been stored— we have given no thought
   to this aspect of the system at present!) If a borrower has the

book at present, then this information, together with the date due for return must be displayed. Otherwise a message that the book should be available on the shelf is required.

3. **Add extra books to the catalogue when they are purchased**

All the details applying to the new books should be entered into the system and then these new items should be added to the catalogue in *the appropriate place*. Notice that here we are caught in rather a difficult situation: since we are aiming to say what should happen without predetermining the way in which the information should be stored, we are not in a position to say how the extra records should be added to the database. On the other hand, until we can predict whereabouts the new items should be added, it may be that we cannot adequately determine how the data should be stored!

4. **Remove lost or damaged books from the catalogue**

This process simply requires that the appropriate records relating to the books to be removed from the catalogue are removed or changed to show that the particular book no longer exists. Notice how we cannot simply say that the record must be removed, since it is possible that the decision will have been taken to have a single record for each title, and have the record listing how many identical copies are stocked. In this case, the requirement will be to reduce the count of the number of copies held, rather than to delete the record!

In each case, we have given a brief description of what the requirement amounts to in practice. At the present time we have given the description in English, and the appropriateness, or otherwise, of this approach is something which we consider later.

3.5.1   Exercise

1. Think about the book issuing system which is needed in a library. Following the approach in the previous section, make a list of the

data requirements and the processing requirements for this sub-system. Finally, give a brief account of each of the processing needs.

2. Look again at the lists of functional and non-functional requirements given in section 3.3. Bearing in mind the specific requirements we have identified in the preceding section and the requirements you identified in the previous exercise, make an expanded list of functional and non-functional requirements which responds to your greater understanding of the problem at this stage.

3.6 Moving on from the specification

So far, we have looked at the requirements of a library system under two broad headings: maintaining the catalogue and dealing with books borrowed and book returns. In each case, we have begun from a consideration of the data which needs to be stored and processed, and have developed our thinking into a series of simple specifications, written in English (a so-called *natural language*) for the procedures which need to be undertaken. This specification of the requirements of the system must now form the basis for the implementation.

3.6.1 Approaches to Implementation

There are a number of different approaches which may be adopted in moving from the sort of informal approach to specifying the requirements of a new system to actually implementing the system specified. There are several factors which have to be considered in determining which approach is appropriate to the particular situation in hand. For example, we might

1. Write a more detailed description of the requirements of each procedure. We might then link together the different procedures to describe the system which is built using an appropriate structured analysis diagram, such as a Jackson's structure diagram. These are described in many books on programming, for example Ford

(1990a). The implementation phase might then consist of proceeding to refine the requirements of each procedure successively until it is simple enough to code. This approach is illustrated in figures 3.1 to 3.4, which relate to the library cataloguing system.

2. We might have been able to identify some sort of applications package which can undertake the operations which we have specified, and therefore the next task might be the installation and detailed configuration of the package to the precise application. In this case the processes involved could be varied according to the way in which packages are configured:

   (a) Some packages require the use of a specialised programming language, in which case a method similar to the one discussed in this book for conventional programming languages would be appropriate

   (b) Some packages are designed to ask the user a series of questions and self-configure on the basis of the answers to the questions.

   (c) Some packages are *freeform* in that they are not especially configurable, but will behave in the required manner if they are given appropriate instructions.

   (d) Some packages will need to be configured by the manufacturer or by a specialist software dealer tied to the manufacturer, in which case it will be important to communicate the specification to the third party in a clear manner in the form required by them.

3. We might have identified a programming language which will form the basis of the implementation. In this case, it might be appropriate to construct more detailed information in a language based closely upon the language selected. Two languages commonly used for such specifications are ADA and Pascal— it is quite common to find detailed specifications expressed in Pseudo Pascal or in a language based upon ADA. Some simple Pseudo Pascal descriptions of procedures are shown in figure 3.5.

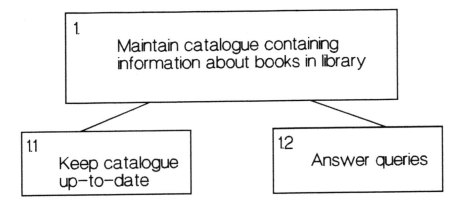

Figure 3.1

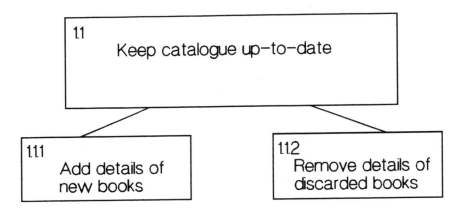

Figure 3.2

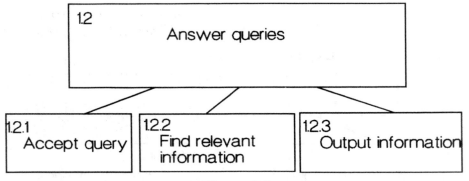

Figure 3.3

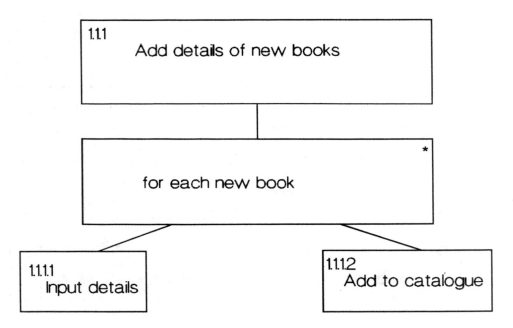

Figure 3.4

The following pseudo Pascal procedures correspond to the processes described in the boxes of the structure diagrams in figures 3.1 - 3.4..

```
Pseudo Pascal
for Figure 3.1
program catalogue

procedure Update
begin

end

procedure Query
begin

end
```

```
Pseudo Pascal
for Figure 3.2
procedure Update

procedure AddBooks;
begin

end

procedure RemoveBooks;
begin

end
```

Figure 3.5a

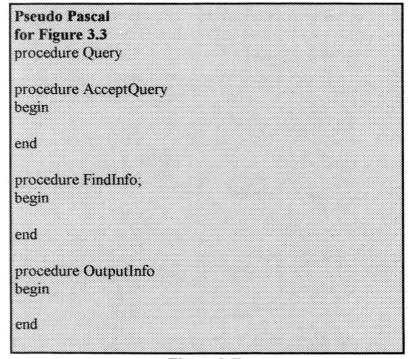

```
Pseudo Pascal
for Figure 3.3
procedure Query

procedure AcceptQuery
begin

end

procedure FindInfo;
begin

end

procedure OutputInfo
begin

end
```

Figure 3.5b

```
Pseudo Pascal
for Figure 3.4 (also continued on next page)
type
        BookRec
        BookFile = File of BookRec
var
        Catalogue, NewBooks: BookFile;

procedure Add(Book: BookRec);
var ThisBook, NextBook:BookRec;
begin
read(Catalogue, Nextbook);
compare(NextBook,Book);
case
        Book < NextBook .AddToHead;
        Book = NextBook: AddDuplicate;
        Book > NextBook: begin
                        while not (eof(Catalogue) or
BookAdded) do
                        begin
                        Thisbook := NextBook;
                        read(catalogue,NextBook);
                        Compare( NextBook, Book);
```

```
             Case
                    Book < NextBook: AddBook;
                    Book= NextBook: AddDuplicate;
                    Book>NextBook: continue
             end;
             end;
             If Not BookAdded then AddToEnd;
      end;
end;
end;

procedure AddBooks
var CurrentBook: BookRec;
begin
while not eof(NewBooks) do
      begin
      read(NewBooks,CurrentBook);
      Add(CurrentBook);
      end;
end.
```

Figure 3.5c

4. We might not yet have identified the medium for implementation, but nevertheless choose to write out the specification in a structured way, based upon the sorts of constructions which we know are commonly provided by computer programming languages. In this case, we might choose to base our language on Pascal or on ADA as in the previous example. Alternatively, however, we would often use a form of *structured English* for the program specifications. This approach has the advantage of being widely understood, because no special language, notation or symbols are used. On the other hand, structured English has the advantage over the use of normal English (the *natural language*) in that the expressions used are carefully selected to offer clear and unambiguous modes of expression. Figure 3.6 shows some simple structured English used in this way.

Each of these methods has its advantages and disadvantages, and we have identified some of these already. All of these methods, however, are based upon fairly well respected approaches to program development, which emphasise the importance of:

- a structured approach to program development

- advanced planning

- a top-down approach to systems development.

We should note, however, that there can be good reasons for the use of a bottom up approach to certain aspects of systems development in certain cases.

In the next chapter, we shall argue that the use of these informal methods of systems specification is fundamentally flawed, and that there are good reasons for rejecting it as an ideal. However, we shall also discover the extent of the problem when we come to try to replace it with a more rigorous approach which we would otherwise favour in all real-life situations. As we shall see, the key issue is involved in the trade-off between the quality of the system being defined and the cost of its definition and implementation.

Structured English specification of a procedure to search for a book in a library catalogue

SEARCH PROCEDURE
1. Look at details of required book
2. Get details of first book in catalogue
3. Compare details of required book with details of current book in catalogue.
    3.1 Details match: book found
    3.2 Required book belongs before current book: book not in library
    3.3 Required book belongs further on: get details of next book in catalogue
4. Repeat 3 until book found or book not in library or no more books in catalogue
5. Report result:
    5.1 book found: display details of where book is kept
    5.2 book not in library: display message reporting book not available

Figure 3.6

3.6.2   Approaches to Specification Validation

Suppose that we are developing a new system to satisfy a management proposal from an organisation. The discussion so far has described how we might go about specifying the requirements of the new system. The techniques which together form the basis of software engineering have as their prime purpose, the intention of increasing the quality of software produced. In order to ensure that this is indeed happening, the requirements specification needs to be subjected to an appraisal of its validity and also the implemented version needs to be verified.

The validation of a system's specification means undertaking four processes (Sommerville (1989)):

- Checking the user's needs and aspirations against the specification. This includes the task of checking that all the user's requirements have been identified.

- Checking that the requirements listed are consistent.

- Checking that the user has identified all the requirements of the system.

- Checking that the requirements listed are realistic.

Thus, we are discussing here the question of whether or not the system has been correctly specified, rather than the quality of the implementation.

The problem which is faced here is that the requirements specification is not always presented in a form which will make it easy to establish whether or not the management and employees who will actually use the system will find it acceptable. We have identified already the limitations of English language as a means for giving a clear and unambiguous description of the specification for a new computerised system. The shortcomings of English in this area lead to the use of pseudo-code and special notational and symbolic devices for the clearest possible description of what is required. This is all very well for communication within the team of software engineers who may all be expected to become conversant with whatever system is in use in a particular project, but it limits the possibility of getting the specification confirmed by the management. The requirements definition document originated from discussions with the management and was for joint consumption by both management and software engineers and we recognised it as being important for this document to be easily understood by both groups. However it is unfortunate if the more detailed description of what should be implemented can then not be examined by the management so that the design can be confirmed.

This leads us to a trade-off between, on the one hand, a well written and clearly, unambiguously presented account of the proposed specification understood by all the professional computer personnel on the project while not understood by management of the organisation for whom the work is to be completed, or, on the other hand, a document which is understood by both parties but which is less satisfactory because it leaves room for misunderstanding. Neither situation is satisfactory, and therefore various suggestions have been made as to how to close the gap.

One possibility, and one which is becoming increasingly important with the advent of more and more high level languages and applications generators, is the use of prototyping. Prototyping is discussed in some detail in chapter 10 of the current work. The aim is to give the client an idea of how a new system will behave. By doing this, both client and software engineers can reach a fuller understanding of the requirements, functions and limitations of the proposed system.

By taking a well-defined requirements definition and developing very rapidly a prototype system which behaves in an appropriate way, there is the possibility for the client to identify problems in the specification at this early stage. This is far more satisfactory than waiting until a full conventional implementation of the system is completed before it becomes possible to identify major flaws in the specification.

Rapid prototyping based on well-defined requirements specifications is therefore an important feature of requirements validation. One might be tempted to ask, if a prototype system may be developed very quickly, why is it still worth the considerable expense of implementing the full system— why not simply use the prototype? The answer to this question depends on a number of factors. In a limited number of situations it may actually be possible to use the prototype in practice, but in most situations it will not. Prototypes commonly run much more slowly than the finally implemented system or are unable to cope with the real requirements of the system under development. For example, the prototype system for a public library might restrict the number of books and borrowers to unrealistically small levels.

It is easy to get the impression that the system requirements definition and specification documents are drawn up and then validated against the user's requirements. Although this does often happen in practice, it is not an approach which is to be commended. It is far more satisfactory for the two processes to work in parallel, with the user being asked to validate at frequent intervals the latest version of the definition and specification documents. This leads to an iterative approach to systems definition and specification and a much greater quality control in the validation of the design.

3.6.3   Approaches to System Testing

Apart from validation of the requirements definition and specification documents, the other major concern for quality control, is over system testing. Where validation refers to checking that the system being designed is the right system to implement, system testing and *verification* is concerned with checking that the system design is being implemented faithfully and acceptably.

There are really two issues at stake here. One is whether the system which has been validated as the appropriate system to implement is being implemented in the appropriate way, and the second is that it is being implemented in a way which is free from mistakes.

For many years, computer software hasd been accused of containing many bugs and errors of implementation. It has been argued that the reason for these problems is that software is inadequately tested. In this section, we consider what is involved in system testing, and how it relates to the requirements definition and specification documents.

One problem with testing a system is that it is usually done by the programmer who has just implemented it. The reason that this might cause problems is that the programmer is likely to test the system according to the programmer's own understanding of the purposes to which the system is to be put. Unfortunately, for reasons which we have already met, the programmer's understanding of the system being implemented is sometimes some distance removed from the system which should be implemented— generally as a result of ambiguous and unclear system specification material. It has therefore been recognised for some time that it should not be for the programmer to specify the way in which the system should be tested, but instead it should be somebody with a clearer understanding of the system design goals.

For these reasons, following the development strategy which we have described here, it makes sense for the requirements specification document to specify the performance goals for the system and the way in which the system should be tested to ensure that it meets these goals. If we think for a moment about this task, things begin to become clear: Since the initial discussions with the management result in the requirements definition, and since this is the document which specifies the functional and non-functional requirements of the proposed system, it is upon these specified requirements that the testing methods should be based. The aim is to have the testing fully specified within the requirements specification before implementation is begun (or even before the implementation method is specified).

Testing at this level is very important and should be completed on the basis of testing each module within a system as well as testing the whole system (which involves testing that the various modules fit together neatly and without problems). Clearly the ideal is to test the system under every conceivable combination of inputs, but this is generally impractical, and, instead, data is selected which represents every possible combination of circumstances to which the system must react. As we shall discuss in the next chapter, system testing which depends upon sampling suitable test data is totally dependent on the system behaving the way we expect. Since we are aiming to test whether or not the system does behave the way we expect, this is a rather unsatisfactory basis on which to perform the testing!

3.7   Exercises

1. Write a specification in natural language (English) for a computer system which deals with customers ordering items from a mail

order catalogue.

2. Show your specification from question 1 to a friend and make a list together of the ambiguities and omissions within your specification.

3. Try to think how a program written to your specification should be tested.

Chapter 4

Formal Methods

4.1   Introduction

In this chapter, we will continue our discussion of software requirements definition and specification from chapters 2 & 3 and we shall begin to discuss some rather more rigorous methods of defining requirements. We shall see that there are many advantages in terms of the quality and confidence that we derive in the software produced when we use these *formal* methods. On the other hand, there are also some overheads which must be taken into account.

4.2   What do we mean by formal methods?

The methods which we discussed in chapter 3 for the definition and specification of software were based, in the main, on natural languages such as English, or on computer languages such as ADA or Pascal. We have already seen how English is less than satisfactory as a means of making clear definitions, because English sentences may be ambiguous. Even when they are totally unambiguous, the language is sometimes misused so that the meaning of particular statements made in English is not clear. The specifications which we have seen written out, based upon either natural languages or computer languages have been *informal* in the way they have described what is going on. The use of the term informal here implies that the ways in which things are described depends to at least some extent on a common understanding of what is written among those people reading the statement. If that assumed common understanding was not in fact present, then the statements would become either meaningless (at best) or ambiguous or incorrect (at worst).

Since this distinction between formal and informal methods of expression is an unfamiliar one for many students of this subject, we shall consider again our case study example of a public library. Consider the statement:

A list of borrowers is to be maintained

This is an informal statement about one of the requirements of our library system, because it assumes that the people who read about the list of borrowers have some sort of understanding already about what is to be done.

In particular, the statement presupposes an understanding of what a *borrower* is, and of what we mean by saying that we will have a *list* of these items, and what we mean by saying that the list of items will be *maintained*.

If we were to try to make some sort of formal definition which would describe the same requirement then we would need to make the following information clear:

- What exactly is a borrower?

- What do we mean by a list?

- What exactly is to be done with the borrowers and the list?

There is no reason why we should not now attempt to make a formal definition of the same requirement based upon the English language (although for reasons which will become more apparent later, English is really not a very good choice for expressing these formal definitions). It might go something like this:

1. A borrower is a person with a name and address

2. A list of things consists of a collection of things stored one after another. There is a first thing in the list and a last thing in the list.

3. To maintain a list, we need to be able to add extra things to the list, remove existing things from the list and find the items on the list and print them out.

This is our first attempt at a formal specification of something, and it is not at all watertight, it could certainly be criticised by somebody reading it:

- What is a person?

- What is a thing?

- What does it mean to say 'there is a first thing in the list'

in fact the collection of possible criticisms which could be aimed at our specification is almost endless. On the other hand, as far as it goes, this more formal specification, even in the restricted form in which it is offered here, does go some way towards avoiding the ambiguity and unclear nature of the original informal statement. Since we are determining more clearly the meaning of more of the terms we are using, the scope for misunderstanding is definitely reduced.

From this example, we can begin to deduce some of the principal features of formal methods:

1. A formal specification makes clear the nature of all the objects to which it refers

2. Objects may be defined in terms of other objects

3. The amount of intuition required to understand the specification is eliminated (in theory at least. Intuition needed to understand the specification may be kept to a minimum in some practical cases)

We may also begin to make a list of some of the problems with the use of formal methods:

1. Formal methods can be clumsy and tedious to use. It can be that some of the statements seem to state the obvious in a very unclear way.

2. However careful we are, we shall always end up defining some entities in terms of others which we have not defined. (See for example, the use of *person* to define *borrower*. It is therefore important that we accept some fundamental categories to form the basis for other definitions

3. We need to be particularly careful with the use of natural language in a formal definition. Terms are used to mean what we have defined them to mean. They no longer have their *intuitive* meaning

4. Some people find a formal definition harder to understand than an informal one (Perhaps this is simply a reflection of the common misuses of language which people make in their speech.)

4.3   Becoming more formal

The use of formal methods in software specification is becoming more widespread in practical cases now, but is still a comparatively recent innovation. As a result, many of the methods and publications on the subject have their roots within research conducted by Computer Scientists rather than in actual practical applications. A number of different techniques and approaches have been developed, and for the purposes of the illustrations in the present work, we have chosen to discuss, in the main, the Vienna Development Method (VDM).

In our discussions so far, we have concerned ourselves with the definition and specification of the requirements of a system in terms of what the system will be able to do. We have not, therefore, been concerned with any discussions of the user interface. This is considered by some software engineers to be an important omission. For our purposes it seems justified, particularly since the VDM method is itself concerned only with the *functional specification* and not with other matters, and the purpose of this book is to introduce the concepts and techniques of formal methods rather than to provide an exhaustive account.

Hekmatpour and Ince (1988) give the following description of the steps involved in VDM

- specify the system formally

- prove that the specification is consistent

- **do**

  - refine and decompose the specification (i.e. produce a *realisation* of the specification)

  - prove that the realisation satisfies the previous specification

- **until** the realisation is as concrete as a program

- revise the above steps

This sequence gives us a much more focused view of the objectives of our formal approach than did our previous discussion. Certainly the use of a formal specification does allow us to give a clear and unambiguous statement of the functional requirements of our system, but there is more to it than that. The very nature of the formal specification allows us, if we are competent in the manipulation of these formal specifications, to transform the specification as written into the statements of a programming language.

But what exactly are the benefits of this transformation? In what ways are the programs developed using this transformation likely to be more satisfactory than the ones we would develop through the more usual techniques?

In the previous chapter we discussed how one might go about judging and verifying the quality of the software which is developed. In that section we discussed the ways in which software could be tested. We took particular note of the importance that software testing methods should form a part of the original specification if quality in software is to be improved. Nevertheless, we had reservations about the software testing process because of the way in which it relies upon the software behaving predictably. In effect, we have to assume that the software meets some quality constraints if our testing is to be accurate!

The VDM method for developing software adopts a different position. Instead of completing the software development and then trying to experiment with different test data to see whether the system performs to specification, as in the usual software development cycle, VDM defines a process whereby each section of the program is *proved* to be correct, because it is developed in a formal and *provable* way from the original specification. Thus, at every stage in the development process, the current specification is decomposed into sub-specifications which are then *proved* to be equivalent to the original.

In this way, the system can be proved to be correct as specified, rather than just demonstrated to work correctly for a particular set of test inputs. In theory, at least, systems developed in this way can be expected to be totally foolproof and to display very high accuracy and quality.

The problem, naturally, is the question of how exactly to prove that specifications are equivalent, one with another, and that requires some discussion of what is meant by the word *proof*. Many books on formal methods begin with a discussion of logic and mathematics before introducing their purpose in terms of program development. We have not done this, because we believe it is important to gain an appreciation of what the purpose of formal methods is before we embark on showing how exactly they are constructed. Nevertheless, we shall need some discussion of some simple mathematics and some appropriate notation as we proceed.

In order to begin to appreciate the fundamental difference between a *proof* and a *test* we shall consider a very simple mathematical equation:

$$2x + 3 = 5$$

Most of you will no doubt be able to solve this mathematically, the sequence of operations goes something like this:

- $2x + 3 = 5$

- Subtract 3 from each side

- $2x = 2$

- Divide each side by 2

- $x = 1$

These steps in the solution of the equation form the basis of a *proof* that if $2x + 3 = 5$, then $x = 1$. In other words, we are certain after following these steps that the **only** solution of the equation is $x = 1$, so long as we can be sure that the rules of elementary algebra can be trusted!

On the other hand, we might have tried to reason as follows:

- Look at the equation $2x + 3 = 5$

- Try $x = 1$ - success! so $x = 1$ is a solution

- Try $x = 2$, $x = 3$, etc. No others work.

- Conclude $x = 1$ is the only solution.

This second 'method' is one which is doomed to failure in general, but happens to succeed in getting the right answer this time! People who understand mathematics would make the following criticisms of the trial and error method:

1. We have looked only at a few positive whole numbers, we do not know whether we should also be looking at fractions, negative numbers or very large numbers as alternative answers.

2. We might have found an answer. But is it **the** answer, or are there in fact lots of answers we have not found. This second method fails to give a satisfactory account of this.

Testing of computer software may not be quite as naive as the trial and error method of solving the equation, but it lays itself open to just the same criticisms. We only test the performance of the software against the inputs where we *predict* that there will be an interesting outcome. We make no attempt to *prove* that the output at non-tested inputs is acceptable.

If we now look in some more detail at the simple mathematical example which we have just discussed, we see that it begins with a specification of a condition: in other words we begin by saying 'What we are looking for is a suitable value of x which will satisfy the equation $2x + 3 = 5$.' At this point in the discussion, we are not concerned with how one might go about actually finding the value of x which we seek, but rather we are interested in *defining* what conditions the sought for value will satisfy when we find it. The series of steps which we have identified then illustrates how we could go about realising our aim and finding the value of x.

In a moment, we shall look at a simple formal definition of a *function*. By analogy with the approach just described, here too we shall begin by making a clear statement of exactly how the function which we require will behave: we will give careful consideration to the questions of

- what the requirements are on the *parameters* on which the function acts, these are known as the *pre-conditions*

- what the requirements are when the function is completed- these are known as the *post-conditions*.

Once we have a clear idea of these pre-conditions and post-conditions, we will then be in a position to know exactly what the function must be able to do. It is from this *implicit* description of the function which we must work to give the *realisation* of the function in its explicit form. In other words, we aim to finish up with a clear cut series of instructions which go to make up the function. These instructions should be provably equivalent to the pre- and post-conditions specified.

4.3.1 Example

In order to keep things as simple as possible, we shall define a very simple mathematical function which multiplies odd integers by 2 and divides even integers by 2. The function is not defined for non-integers.

We shall begin by posing three questions:

1. What does the function do? To be precise, what sort of things does it act upon (what is its *domain*) and what sort of answers does it give (what is its *co-domain*).

2. What are the pre-conditions, if any?

3. What are the post-conditions, if any?

For the present, we shall call our function f, and we shall answer the questions in order:

1. f is a function defined on those real numbers which are integers and it gives an answer which is a real number (and happens also to be an integer). We shall consider f as a function from real numbers to real numbers. This is written as follows:

$$f(x : \text{real})y : \text{real}$$

In other words, the function f takes as its input the value x which is a real number and gives as output the value y which is also a real number.

2. The pre-condition for the function f is that the real number x must in fact be an integer. We shall express this in the form:

$$PRE\ x \in Z$$

which uses some shorthand notation, notably the Z to represent the set of all integers (whole numbers) and the symbol $\in$ to represent the words *is a member of*.

3. Finally, we need to give the post condition, which says that if x is odd then $y = 2 \times x$ and if x is even then $y = x/2$. Again we have a special way of writing this down:

$$POST\ \{(x\ \text{even}) \wedge (y = x/2)\} \vee \{(x\ \text{odd}) \wedge (y = 2 \times x)\}$$

The special symbols used here are $\wedge$ for **and** and $\vee$ for **or**. We may therefore read the formal statement in the following way: 'POST condition: either x is even and $y = x/2$ or x is odd and $y = 2 \times x$'

This implicit specification looks as though it is rather long-winded, but this is really only because we are trying to understand what is going on as we write it down. In practice, the formal specification of the function f in the above form would simply say:

$$f(x : \text{real})y : \text{real}$$

$$PRE \ x \in Z$$

$$POST \ \{x \text{ even} \land (y = x/2)\} \lor \{x \text{ odd} \land (y = 2 \times x)\}$$

To work from this formal definition of the function f to a *realisation* of the function f (i.e. a description of how it might be implemented) we shall need to show that:

For every real number x which satisfies the pre-condition for f, the value y output by f satisfies the post-condition.

In other words, to prove that we have realised the function f in its formal specification, it will be insufficient to consider simply some appropriate test data and work on the basis that if f tests accurately, then it must be accurate. Instead, we shall aim to *prove* that the realisation of f satisfies its specification exactly.

Before we attempt to complete this proof, look again at the statement of the proof required. This statement makes explicit the role of the pre-condition when it comes to the realisation of the function. For the proof is concerned *only with those values of x which satisfy the pre-condition*. For any value of x which does not satisfy the pre-condition of f, we have no information specifying the output, y.

To begin with, we present an explicit realisation of the function f:

$$f(x)\underline{\Delta} \text{ if } x \text{ even then } x/2 \text{ else } x \times 2.$$

To prove that this expression for f is indeed a realisation of the specification, we proceed as follows:

1. $x \in Z$ (Pre-condition)

2. x is even or x is odd (Property of Z)

3. **from** x is even (Case 1)

   (a) $y = x/2$ (Specification)
   (b) **infer** if x is even then $y = x/2$

4. **from** x is odd (Case 2)

   (a) $y = 2 \times x$ (Specification)

5. **infer** if x is even the $y = x/2$ else $y = x \times 2$

This proves that the given realisation is valid.

4.3.2 Example

We shall now consider a second mathematical example of a formal specification. This time, we will work more directly to the specification, and we will then prove that we have an appropriate realisation of the given specification.

Define the function M by the following:

$M(x : \text{real})y : \text{real}$
PRE: True
POST: $\{(y = x) \lor (y = -x)\} \land (y \geq 0)$

Notice here how the pre-condition is 'True' which implies that the specification must hold for all real values of x.

We claim that the following definition of $M(x)$ gives a valid realisation of this specification:

$M(x)\underline{\Delta}$ if $x > 0$ then x else $-x$

and we proceed to prove this:

Proof:

1. $x \in R$

2. $x > 0$ or $x \leq 0$

3. $\{(y = x) \vee (y = -x)\} \wedge \{y \geq 0\}$

4. **from** $x > 0$

    (a) $\{(y = x) \wedge (y \geq 0)\} \vee \{(y = -x) \wedge (y \geq 0)\}$

    (b) $\{(y = x) \wedge (y \geq 0)\} \vee \{False\}$

    (c) **Infer** $(y = x)$

5. **from** $x \leq 0$

    (a) $\{(y = x) \wedge (y \geq 0)\} \vee \{(y = -x) \wedge (y \geq 0)\}$

    (b) $\{False\} \vee \{(y = -x) \wedge (y \geq 0)\}$

    (c) **Infer** $(y = -x)$

6. If $x > 0$ then $y = x$ else $y = -x$

4.3.3   Example

Having looked at two mathematical examples of formal specification, we shall now consider an example drawn from data processing. The example will, of necessity, be a straightforward one, but it will begin to illustrate how the methods which we have just met might be applied in practice:

This example is concerned with a Bank ATM cash dispenser machine. These machines will be familiar to many readers. Bank customers use a plastic card which has a magnetic identification strip attached to it. This card is inserted into the machine and the customer types in a Personal Identification Number (PIN). The cash dispenser machine checks with the stored PIN number list to ensure that the correct number has been entered, to match the inserted card before either giving a menu of options or rejecting the customer as an imposter.

Here we will consider the function which the machine uses to distinguish between a real customer and an imposter. We will start with an informal description of the function and then proceed first to a formal specification (which is implicit) and finally to a proof that the implicit representation can lead to an explicit realisation.

Informally, we will consider the function *Truecustomer* to take a Plastic card and a PIN number and determine whether the entered PIN number identifies the user of the card as the true customer of the bank.

We shall write our formal specification as follows:

Truecustomer(x:plastic card, y:PIN number)z:{True,False}

PRE: x belongs to correct bank

POST: $\{$match$(x,y) \wedge (z = $true$)\} \vee \{($not match$(x,y)) \wedge (z = $false$)\}$

Notice how these specifications depend upon a function *match* already having been set up. This function *match* is assumed to give a *true* value if the card x and the PIN number y are compatible and a false value otherwise. We will not at this stage attempt a formal specification of the function *match*.

A possible realisation of the function *Truecustomer* could be expressed as follows:

Truecustomer(x,y) $\underline{\Delta}$ if match(x,y) then true else false.

The proof that this realisation is satisfactory is straightforward:

1. x=plastic card, y=PIN number

2. (match(x,y)=true) $\vee$ (match(x,y)=false)

3. **from** match(x,y)=true

    (a) (match(x,y) = true) $\wedge$ (z=true)

    (b) **infer** if match(x,y)= true then z = true

4. **from** match(x,y) = false

    (a) (match(x,y) = false) $\wedge$ (z = false)

    (b) **infer** if match(x,y)=false then z = false

5. (if match(x,y)=true then z = true) $\wedge$ (if match(x,y)=false then z = false)

6. if match(x,y)=true then true else false

which completes the proof.

4.3.4 Exercises

1. Define the function Square as follows: Square(x:real) y:real

   PRE: True

   POST: $y = x^2$ Prove that the following is a valid realisation of

   this function:

   Square(x) $\underline{\Delta}$ $x \times x$

2. Define the function Sign as follows:

   Sign(x:real)y : $\{+1, -1\}$

   PRE: $x \neq 0$

   POST:$\{(x > 0) \wedge (y = +1)\} \vee \{(x < 0) \wedge (y = -1)\}$ Prove that

   the following is a direct definition of the sign function:

   Sign(x) $\underline{\Delta}$ if $x > 0$ then $+1$ else -1.

3. Here is a specification for the (real) square root function *Root*:

   Root(x:Real)y:Real

   PRE: $x \geq 0$

   POST: $(y^2 = x) \wedge (y \geq 0)$

   Why do we need the pre-condition in this case?

   Prove that the following is a valid explicit form for the function
   root.

   Root(x) $\underline{\Delta}$ $+\sqrt{x}$

4. Here is a specification for the function which checks the catalogue
   in a library for a book required:

   Search(Searchitem:Title, Catalogue:List of books):Result:{True,False}

PRE: True

POST: $\{(\text{Searchitem} \in \text{Catalogue}) \wedge (\text{Result=True})\} \vee \{(\text{Searchitem} \notin \text{Catalogue}) \wedge (\text{Result} = \text{False})\}$

Prove the validity of the following realisation of this function:

$\text{Search}(x,y) \triangleq$ if $x \in y$ then **True** else **False**.

4.4 Input-Processing-Output Specifications?

We note how the use of formal specification techniques in the form we have met them so far encourages the software engineer to work in an implementation-free way while designing the requirements definition and specification documents. This is because we are encouraged to consider *implicit* definitions of the function, rather than to concentrate on the way in which the functions shall be realised. This fits well with an approach to systems design which the author has always promoted and which may be found useful:

Traditionally, we are encouraged to consider a data processing system as being concerned with three stages: input, processing and output (See figure 4.1). This encourages the software engineer or systems analyst to approach the problem of designing new systems in precisely this way: consider the form of the data which goes in, consider what processing is needed and then determine the output. This approach makes it fairly easy to see how an existing system works.

On the other hand, this approach tends to encourage a belief that the existing system in operation is a good basis for future developments, and this is by no means always the case. It may be helpful therefore to consider an alternative approach to examining a system. Figure 4.2 illustrates this alternative approach, which views the outputs of the system as being paramount. Presumably all the data which is collected, input, processed and stored is used because of the desire to produce some form of output. Therefore a list of the desired outputs will lead naturally to a consideration of the necessary inputs and processing required to enable the outputs to be produced.

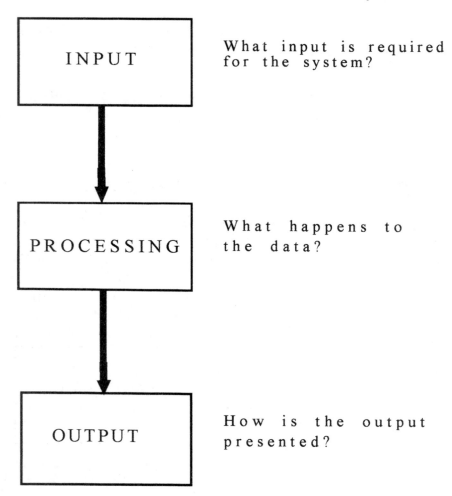

Figure 4.1 View of a data processing system as considered in
conventional systems analysis

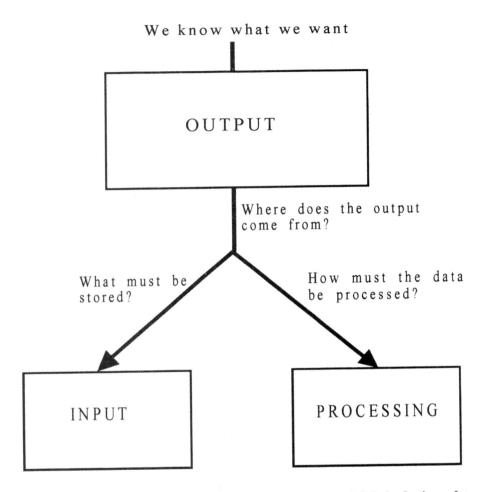

Figure 4.2 View of a data processing system which is designed to produce specified outputs.

The formal design system which we have just met reflects this alternative approach, since we are concerned with defining the pre- and post-conditions before even considering how the processing will happen. These conditions simply specify the output expected and when it should arise. The same pre- and post-conditions could be satisfied by a variety of different approaches to implementation.

Chapter 5

Becoming less explicit

5.1   Introduction

In this chapter we shall be considering the merits of implicit and explicit definitions of functions and procedures. Experienced programmers often find it difficult to work with implicit specifications, which
are nevertheless often to be preferred. We shall see that explicit definitions can appeal more naturally to experienced programmers. We
shall then assess how explicit and implicit approaches influence the implementation and realisation of the application, and we shall discuss
alternatives. Finally, we shall look at the ways in which simple implicit
and explicit specifications of a problem can be realised in appropriate
high level languages.

5.2   Specifications: What are we trying to do?

To begin with, it is important to have a clear understanding of just what
it is that we are trying to do. Specifying a problem involves producing
an unambiguous description of what a solution to the problem should
accomplish. Expressing this in terms of ideas which we met in the
previous chapter, we need to write down the pre- and post- conditions
using a suitable language which is free from ambiguity and which is

generally understood by those who need to use it. We have already understood that the use of a formal rather than informal language for this is preferable since it removes much of the possibility for ambiguity.

In chapter 2, we identified some of the features which go to make a good specification. Among these, apart from the obvious requirement that the specification is clear and correct, was the demand that the specification should be implementation independent. In other words, the specification should define what it is that we are trying to do, but without presuming to describe how it is that the job is to be done.

Unfortunately, this desire to be implementation independent is rather a difficult one to satisfy, because it is extremely difficult for an experienced software designer (programmer, analyst, or software engineer) to be really detached from the project, and to take a truly unbiased view when specifying a new system. It is only natural that opinions of just what it is that a system should be able to do will be influenced by previous experiences of similar systems which worked and of others which were less satisfactory. We meet exactly the same tendency in everyday life when we ask a friend to describe the appropriate route to follow to a particular place, and we are treated to a detailed description of the traffic jams we are likely to encounter.

But really, all we are interested in at this stage is a description of what the solution should do. The decision as to how to implement the solution and to produce the program must be left until a later stage. This is because the decisions about how to implement should be informed by the detailed description of what it is that must be implemented. The danger is, that the sooner the implementation method is determined the more likely it is that the desired implementation will influence the definition of what it is that we should implement.

In other words, if we decide to write a program using the language Pascal, we shall continuously be comparing our requirements with the capabilities of Pascal. In doing this, we will avoid writing down requirements which are inappropriate to a program which will be written in Pascal. The result of this is that the specification does not describe the real need, but rather how we might program the solution in Pascal. This is clearly a very restrictive approach.

5.3 Explicit specifications

In the previous chapter, we met the concept of pre and post- conditions, and we investigated how they may be applied to appropriate problems to specify what needs to happen in a procedure.

In order to reach an understanding of how Pre- and Post- conditions may reflect either an explicit or an implicit description, we return to consider the solution of the simple mathematical equation:

$$2x + 3 = 5$$

for all possible solutions which are positive integers.

Now we can probably solve this equation for ourselves. We know

$$2x + 3 = 5$$

so, by subtracting 3 from both sides of the equation, we have

$$2x = 2$$

and then by dividing both sides of the equation by 2, we obtain

$$x = 1.$$

In fact, this process has shown quite conclusively that $x = 1$ is the *only* solution of the equation

$$2x + 3 = 5.$$

Now, we could write this solution out implicitly or explicitly.
An *explicit* statement might look like this

Pre x $\in$ Z Post x = 1

Here, the work has been done, the equation has been solved and we have an *explicit* expression for the value of x which will satisfy the required equation.

On the other hand, we might have written an alternative, *implicit*, expression which defines what it is that we are doing:

Pre x $\in$ Z Post 2x+3=5 The implicit expression describes accurately

and unambiguously exactly what it is that we are trying to find, but doesn't at this stage prescribe what the answer is, nor how we might go about finding it.

5.3.1 Which is better: to be explicit or to be implicit?

If we examine the above example, we can observe several advantages of the explicit definition over the implicit one. For example, the explicit definition gives the answer to the problem, it involves no further work, and the answer is explicitly stated and clearly to be seen. On the other hand, this explicitness also has disadvantages. Only the answer is given, and there is no hint of the problem which is being solved. Therefore the chances of checking that the answer given is correct, or that it is the *only* answer to the problem are removed. In practice it may be an advantage to express the implicit definition since it gives more information to the reader.

5.4 A data processing example

If we return to consider the problem of the bank ATM machine which we discussed in the previous chapter, then we will see that the discussion of the specification of the procedure Truecustomer was expressed in an implicit way. Truecustomer was defined in terms of the question of whether or not the PIN number entered matched the PIN number which was stored by the computer system to correspond to the card which had been entered.

Truecustomer(x:plastic card, y:PIN number)z:{True,False}

PRE: x belongs to correct bank

POST: $\{\text{match}(x,y) \wedge (z = \text{true})\} \vee \{(\text{not match}(x,y)) \wedge (z = \text{false})\}$

An explicit description of the same procedure would be possible, but would involve us in considering more than just the question of what it was that has to be done. In order to give an explicit specification, we need to consider in some detail *how* the task is to be accomplished and then we must describe *what is to be done*.

Thus explicit definitions and specifications can only be written when the writer has an understanding of more than just what the problem is: also needed is an understanding of the sorts of methods which would be used to solve it, and an appreciation of how one such method would be employed in practice, and the outcome.

In the current case, we might need to consider, for example, the question of how the PIN numbers are stored by the computer, how the appropriate one is to be located, and then the question of what is to be done if the number input matches the number stored, and what is to be done if the two numbers do not match. The explicit specification therefore involves more thought and is typically longer than the implicit specification.

On the other hand, it is likely that many people reading this book would naturally start to write an explicit rather than an implicit definition of the problem. Given the same ATM problem to solve, a typical English description of the requirements would run as follows:

The customer enters the card and PIN number and the computer looks the PIN number up on a list to check that the correct PIN number has been entered

But this description is *not an implicit one*, since it begins to presume certain facts about the implementation. For example, the computer is assumed to hold the PIN numbers in a list. No indication is given about the nature of the list, but the use of the word does imply that the data is to be stored in a linear data structure, rather than a multi-dimensional table, and it certainly implies that the data is stored and looked up rather than calculated. Perhaps it doesn't matter that such assumptions are made. Certainly this may be true in the present example, since the data in question does tend to be stored in something very like a list when existing similar systems have been implemented. But as a general rule, we should not allow assumptions, however natural they may seem, and however much they may be informed by previous experience, to influence the actual implementation in the present case.

It is precisely this type of explicitness which creeps in in an unobtrusive way and which can spoil the quality of computer software, either by retaining inappropriate properties of previous similar software in a new system, or by perpetuating the use of inappropriate techniques when programming with a new language or in a new way.

5.5   Why choose an implicit specification?

If we think in detail about the problem of defining the function Truecustomer, then we shall easily observe that the use of an explicit definition will result in a much longer and less clear definition than will the implicit one. Generally, being explicit will yield one of two results:

Either the problem is solved and simplifies to an explicit statement of the answer (as in the case of $2x + 3 = 5$ becoming $x = 1$). In this case, the temptation to be explicit is one which is hard to resist.

But in most cases, the temptation to be explicit causes the description to lose clarity and precision. The explicit description may well be equally accurate, but it contains so much detail that it becomes impossible to identify the fundamental issues which would usually be highlighted in an implicit definition.

A clear example of this arises in route planning. An implicit description of the journey from Chester to Dover might say 'go via London' while an explicit description would consist of a list of road numbers. For the person following the instructions exactly, the explicit description would be more thorough, but would be of no assistance at all if one of the roads listed was closed. In this case the person with the implicit description 'go via London' could easily look at a map and choose an alternative route.

In addition to being shorter, easier to establish and more versatile than an explicit specification, implicit specifications have a number of other advantages. Jones (1990) identifies the following:

1. An implicit specification may reveal a variety of different implementation techniques (as we saw in the variety of routes from Chester to Dover)

2. Properties of the required output may be given in a way which is more understandable to the user

3. An explicit method is usually described in terms of an algorithm. Algorithms always yield a particular result, which may not be equivalent to the specification (but may just be one possible interpretation of it). This is particularly likely to happen when there is more than one possible solution to a problem. Algorithms will usually return a single answer without indicating either the existence or the nature of any alternative answers. With an explicit definition it may therefore be that the most appropriate answers to a particular problem are lost.

4. Pre-conditions are often more explicitly stated in implicit definitions than in explicit ones. Thus, the original problem to solve $(2x + 3 = 5)$ can be lost in the explicit definition of the solution $(x = 1)$ and so it may become more likely that the overall objectives are lost and work concentrates on particular details rather than the general features.

5.6   Types of implementation media

For most programmers, analysts and software engineers, the question of whether or not the original specification is written in an implicit or an explicit way is largely irrelevant, at least at the point when the programs come to be written. Programs written in conventional high level languages need to be designed by describing the solution in terms of an algorithm or method and then the algorithm must be converted into high level programming language statements. (See figure 5.1)

The use of formal methods allows the algorithm to be shown to be provably equivalent (and *proved* to be so) to the original specification, and as we saw in the previous chapter, it should then be possible to prove the fianl realisation of the program as being correct (i.e. satisfying its specification exactly).

The question of just how explicit the original specification is becomes really more a matter of just where we are in the spectrum which

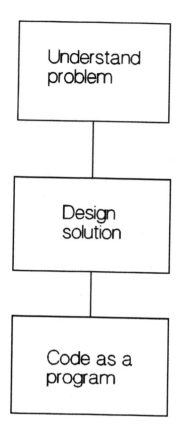

Figure 5.1

ranges from a totally implicit definition of the problem at the one extreme to a totally concrete explicit program at the other. The discussion earlier in this chapter indicates some of the advantages of the definition being made in an implicit way, but the programmer, analyst or software engineer should be in a position to realise the solution no matter what the starting point.

On the other hand, some applications programs are developed today using a completely different style of programming language. Decalarative languages, such as Prolog, do not adopt the algorithmic or procedural approach which is common to conventional programming languages. Figure (5.2) indicates the stages which have to be followed in writing a program using a declarative language and it is clear that it is fundamentally important that the programmer has a clear idea of what the program has to do. On the other hand it is not necessary that the programmer defines the methods to be used in executing the program since this part of the task is undertaken by the language itself.

It has been observed in practice that programmers experienced in writing programs in a conventional high level procedural programming language do not always adapt easily to the very different rigours of writing programs in a declarative language. This is for precisely the same reasons that we have identified in this chapter. It is difficult for experienced programmers to write implicit definitions. When a programmer is experienced in writing programs through developing algorithms, it can often be easier to see how to describe the *methods* required to solve the problem than it is to give *a clear statement of just what the problem is.*

A more detailed discussion of these issues as they relate to developing programs in different languages is given by Ford (1990a). For the present, we shall consider two problems. In each case we shall begin with an informal description of the problem. We shall then develop a formal specification, using VDM and indicate how these specifications might be realised using appropriate high level languages.

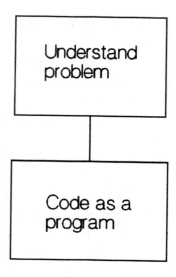

Figure 5.2

5.7   Worked Example 1.

In this first example, imagine that we are choosing a ladies netball team from a large group of 100 students, male and female. This will turn out to be a very good example of when an implicit specification is far easier to produce and more useful than an explicit one.

If we consider, for a moment, the requirements of the example, we can begin to formulate the specification. In order to construct a ladies netball team, then we need to find seven ladies to play. It is clear that this can only be possible if there are at least seven ladies in the population of 100 people from whom the team is to be chosen. This gives us a PRE-condition.

To distinguish between an implicit and an explicit specification of the process, the two questions which we will ask are:

- What does the final solution look like?

- How would we expect to go about finding the solution?

The first of these questions leads us to the implicit specification (figure 5.3). The implicit specification makes the following observations about the solution:

- There are seven members of the team (which we shall call y).

- Each of the seven members of the team is different from each of the other six.

- Each of the seven members of the team is female

Clearly this implicit specification makes no attempt to indicate how such a program might be written.

If we turn now to the question of an explicit specification, we shall be constructing the specification from the answer to the question *How would we expect to go about finding the solution?* In this case (figure 5.3) we can see that one possible explicit specification requires that a team of seven people is selected, any men in the team are replaced, and the process is repeated until all team members are female.

Selection of a ladies netball team - implicit specification

Team(x: list of 100 students)y: list of 7 students
PRE: x contains at least 7 female students
1. POST: $\forall y_1, y_2 \in y: (y_1 \neq y_2) \wedge (y_1 \text{ is female}) \bigcap (y \subset x)$

Selection of a ladies netball team - explicit specification

Team(x: list of 100 students)y: list of 7 students
PRE: x contains at least 7 female students
POST:
        For each element of y:
            repeat
                choose a member, z, of x
           until (z is female)
                and (z is not a member of y)
           put z into current element of y

Figure 5.3

```
program LadiesTeam(input,output,People);
const
    TeamSize = 7;
type
    NameType=array[1..30] of char;
    SexType=(Male,Female);
    Person:    record
            name:NameType;
            sex: SexType
            end;
    TeamType = array[1..TeamSize] of NameType;
var
    People: File of Person;
    Team:TeamType;

procedure InitTeam;
var i : integer;
begin
for i := 1 to TeamSize do
    begin
    Team[i] := 'Insufficient players          ';
    end;
end;
```

Figure 5.4 (Continued on next page)

```pascal
procedure FindTeam;
var
    PlayersFound: integer;
    Player : Person;
begin
PlayersFound := 0;
Reset(People);
while (PlayersFound < TeamSize)
    and (not eof(People)) do
    begin
    read(People,Player);
    if Player.Sex = Female then
        begin
        PlayersFound := PlayersFound + 1;
        Team[PlayersFound] := Player.Name;
        end;
    end;
end;
procedure OutPutTeam;
var
    i:integer;
begin
for i := 1 to TeamSize do
    begin
    writeln('Player ', i, ' ', Team[i]);
    end;
end;
begin
InitTeam;
FindTeam;
OutPutTeam;
end.
```

Figure 5.4
Turbo Pascal program for selecting a Netball team

```
domains
    person = symbol
    team = person*
predicates
    male(person)
    female(person)
    netballteam(team)
    allfemale(team)
    alldistinct(team)
    member(person,team)
    size(team,integer)
clauses
    male(Andrew)
    male(Fred)
    female(Angela)
    male(George)
    female(Ruth)
    female(Sarah)
    male(John)
    female(Abigail)
    male(Pete)
    male(Zechariah)
    male(Paul)
    female(Susan)
    male(Boris)
    female(Queenie)
    male(Roger)
    female(Robin)
    male(Alex)
    female(Paula)
```

Figure 5.5 (Continued on next page)

```
member(X,[X|_])
member(X,[_|H]) :-
        member(X,H)
size([],0)
size([X| RestofTeam],Y):-
        size(RestofTeam)+1,
        not(member(X,RestofTeam))
allfemale([Z]) :-
        female(Z)
allfemale([Z|RestofTeam]):-
        female[Z]
        allfemale(RestofTeam)
alldistinct([X])
alldisctinct(X|RestofTeam):-
        not(member(X,RestofTeam))
        alldistinct(RestofTeam)
netballteam(W):-
        alldistinct(W)
        allfemale(W)
        size(W,7)

goal:   netballteam(X)
```

Figure 5.5
Turbo Prolog program for selecting a Netball team

Figure 5.4 contains a Pascal program which follows the explicit specification and constructs a team of seven women for the netball team. Notice how this program also satisfies the implicit specification, since it must do so to provide a solution to the problem. The Prolog program in figure 5.5 is possibly even more interesting, since it indicates how a Prolog program may be constructed directly from the implicit specification. The Prolog program *does not satisfy* the explicit specification.

All this indicates the danger of writing an explicit specification, since it pre-supposes a particular approach to implementation which may not be the one which should be used.

5.8   Worked Example 2.

In this example, we consider the calculation of an individual's tax and national insurance liabilities, based on tax allowances and contribution rates. We shall see how, in this case, it is almost impossible to be anything other than explicit in the specification.

Following the previous scheme, figure 5.6 gives a specification, and figure 5.7 & 5.8 illustrate the implementation in Pascal and in Prolog.

5.9   Being implicit can be more natural

For most of this chapter, we have assumed that the most natural way for experienced programmers to try to express their specifications is with an explicit definition, and that the use of implicit specification is unnatural. This is undoubtedly true in much of the work of programmers and others involved in the software design process. However it is *sometimes* more natural to describe outcomes implicitly rather than explicitly.

In worked example 1 above, we met a particular case where implicitness was the more natural way of describing our solution, and where, in addition, the implicit description led to a very straightforward program written in an appropriate language.

In other circumstances, the implicit description of the outcome is not only preferable, but it can be the only feasible way to proceed:

Specifications of tax liabilities - explicit

Tax liability = (income - allowances)(basic rate)
            + (income - higher rate level)(higher rate-basic rate)

Specification of tax liabilities - implicit

liabilities(income: integer)y liability:integer
PRE : true
POST liability=(income-allowances)(basic rate)+(income-
            higher rate level)(higher rate-basic rate)

Figure 5.6

```
program tax(input,output);
const
    Allowance = 2400;
    HigherRateLevel = 30000;
    BasicRate = 0.3;
    HigherRate = 0.4;
var
    income,tax:integer;
begin
writeln('What  is your annual income?');
readln(income);
tax := round((income - Allowance)*BasicRate + (income -
        HigherRateLevel)*(HigherRate-BasicRate));
writeln('Your tax liability is: ', tax);
end
```

Figure 5.7 Turbo Pascal to calculate tax liabilities

```
    domains

    predicates
tax(integer,integer)
allowances(integer)
higherratelevel(integer)
basicrate(real)
higherrate(real)
    clauses
allowance(2400)
higherratelevel(30000)
basicrate(0.3)
higherrate(0.4)
tax(X,Y):-
    allowance(A)
    higherratelevel(HRL)
    basicrate(BR)
    higherrate(HR)
    Y= (X-A)*BR + (X-HRL)*(HR-BR)

Goal: tax(income,X)
```

Figure 5.8 Turbo Prolog program to calculate tax liabilities

Mathematicians define the process of integration as the inverse operation of differentiation. Therefore a function can be integrated only if we can find another function which, when differentiated, yields the given function. This is clearly the basis for an implicit, rather than an explicit, definition.

The police can use a database when investigating a crime. Again, they will describe the suspect they are looking for in terms of the attributes which the person should display, rather than in terms of the explicit processes which should be used to find them.

5.10   Exercises

1. A mathematician is asked to solve the equation

$$x^2 + 3x + 2 = 0$$

   Write an implicit specification of the solution.

2. Write an implicit specification for a program which takes a list of names and returns as output the name which is alphabetically first in the list.

3. Write an implicit specification for a computer dating program which chooses a suitable female partner for a male applicant.

4. For each of the above exercises, try to write an explicit specification.

Chapter 6

Induction and Recursion

6.1   Introduction

In this chapter, we shall discuss a technique which is fundamental to the production of many sophisticated computer programs, recursion. Recursion involves the definition of a function or procedure in terms of itself. When we try to specify and realise recursive functions and procedures, we shall find that the methods we have already discussed fail to make a convincing proof, and we need to apply new methods. The simple mathematical technique, known as induction, may be used to show that recursive specifications are satisfied. This method is introduced here and we indicate some of the many advantages of recursive approaches to programming and see how mathematical induction may be used to prove the satisfiability of some realisations of simple recursive procedures.

6.2   What is recursion?

Recursion is, quite simply, the definition of a function or procedure in terms of itself. It is a technique which we all use when describing how something should be done, but we often use the method without even realising that we are using it.

For example, if we are asked to explain how two numbers, each with two digits should be added together (for example, 35 + 47), then we would say 'Add the 5 and the 7, making 12 and write down the units digit, 2. Then add the 3 and the 4 and the 1 which we *carried* to give the tens digit of 8. So the answer is 82'

Although this description is of a simple everyday technique, it applies recursion. This is because the description of how to perform the process of addition requires knowledge of how to add up! Admittedly, we are using the knowledge of how to add single digit numbers to explain how to add two digit numbers. Therefore the recursive explanation in this case is typical of recursive definitions in general, because they apply a simple known method to explain how to undertake a more complicated problem.

6.3   Recursion from a programmer's perspective

In order to set the scene for the present discussion, it is important that we understand how important recursive techniques can be to a programmer. We shall therefore consider how a particular applications program might be written.

In common with our earlier discussion, we shall consider a simple data processing problem to illustrate the method. Sorting a set of data records into a particular order is commonly required in data processing applications.

If we want to write a program to sort a list of 10 names into order, then there are various different ways we could go about it. We could, for example, store all the names in an array, and then apply some algorithmic method to the problem. Bubble sorts, shell sorts and quick sorts are standard algorithms which can be found in books and used to write a program directly.

On the other hand, it is possible to write a recursive procedure to sort a list of names. Remember that a recursive procedure describes how to do something in terms of itself. So, in this case, a recursive procedure will need to describe how to sort a set of names into order, by assuming we have already understood how to sort a simpler set of names into order. In fact, we shall make our definition based on the assumption that a function already exists which performs the sorting!

This all sounds rather strange if you haven't met recursive ideas before, so if this is a new idea to you and seems like cheating, then don't worry, because all will become clearer as we proceed.

To begin with, we can observe that the problem of sorting just one name into order is simple. Therefore if we can reduce the problem of sorting ten names into order into this last problem of sorting a single name, then there will be nothing more to do. We now consider how we might do the sorting job by hand. Imagine that you had a list of ten names, then how would you sort it into order?

One possibility is that you work through the list and find the first name and write that down, deleting it from the original list. A second 'pass' through the list can then be used to locate the second name and so on (figure 6.1).

This method forms the basis for a recursive definition of a sorting method, because we can observe that the method fundamentally consists of finding the first name in the alphabetical order, and then proceding to sort the remaining shorter list. This means that we could define the algorithm as follows. We start with a list of names which contains n names.

```
Sort (names:list, n:integer)
begin
if n = 1 then the list is in order already
        else
        begin
                Find first name
                Sort (names-first name, n-1)
        end
end
```

This recursive algorithmic definition shows that to sort ten names, we find the first name and then sort the remaining nine. To sort the nine names, we use the same method. In other words, we find the first name and then sort the remaining eight, and so on. Finally, to sort the two names, we find the first and sort the remaining one. But a single name is already sorted, so we've finished.

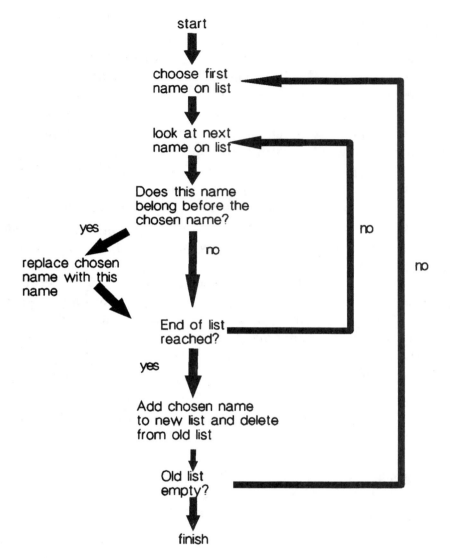

Figure 6.1

It is easy to convert the above algorithm into a program (see appendix I) which uses the same recursive idea.

Many other data processing problems can be solved using recursion, and therefore we are justified in spending some time considering how the formal specification ideas and methods can assist in developing recursive programs.

6.4 Why would we use recursion rather than programming directly?

Having introduced the idea of recursion, which is apparently a very strange method of writing particular procedures, it becomes sensible to consider why programmers should choose to write a procedure or function recursively.

Recursion is well-suited to some problems and totally unsuited to others. Most procedures and functions are better written directly, and only in certain cases is a recursive approach to be prefered. We are able to consider some general rules which help us todetermine when a recursive approach is particularly appropriate in the next subsection.

However for those applications where recursion is appropriate, we can identify from experience the following particular advantages of recursive techniques over direct methods.

1. Recursive programs are typically shorter than their direct counterparts.

2. Recursive programs can be debugged more easily than directly written programs. We can see how this happens if we consider what we actually do as the programmer of a recursive definitions. We begin by defining the way in which the procedure or function should behave for particular simple cases. Then we show how a more complicated case may be built up from the simple cases. Therefore the only detailed programming which needs to be checked is

   - for the simplest case

- for the linking together of simple cases to form the more complex cases.

However, it can take some time for the uninitiated reader of a program to appreciate how a program which has been designed and written recursively actually works.

3. For the same reasons, programs written recursively are less prone to errors.

4. Programs written recursively may take less time to develop.

6.5 How can we recognise when recursion will help?

Generally, recursion can help us when we are trying to solve a problem which would be easy to solve in a simple case (perhaps with very few items to deal with) but which is harder to solve when there are many items. The aim, as we have identified, is to express the general problem in terms of a simpler problem, and then to use the recursive technique to simplify successively until the problem becomes simple enough to solve directly.

Jones (1990) gives a number of arithmetical examples of recursive definitions of functions, and the reader may find it useful to study these. For our purposes, we shall consider one of these examples. Unfortunately, the example chosen is not particularly useful as an applications program, since a recursive definition of *how to multiply positive whole numbers* would be unlikely to be an appropriate application of recursion in practice. A direct definition of multiplication would be more satisfactory. Nevertheless, the discussion of recursion and induction in these familiar contexts will inform our later description of more useful and complex situations.

6.6 Multiplication

If we did not know already how to multiply two arbitrary positive whole numbers together, then we might find a recursive definition useful.

We all know how to multiply any whole number by the number one and we can consistently obtain the correct answer. This can therefore be used as the basis of a recursive definition.

mult(a,b:N)ans:N
  if b = 1 then ans = a else ans = mult(a,b-1)+a
We shall consider this definition in more detail:
  If we wish to evaluate 7×5, we attempt mult(7,5)
  ans = mult(7,4)+7
      = (mult(7,3)+7) +7
      = ((mult(7,2)+7) +7) +7
      = (((mult(7,1)+7) +7) +7)+7
      = (((7 +7) +7) +7) +7
      = 35

Later, we shall see how these ideas are expressed using VDM, but before we do this, we shall need to discuss the mathematical technique known as induction.

6.7 What is different about recursion?

We have met recursive definitions here as being definitions which allow a function or procedure to be described in terms of itself. One of the features which this allows is for us to have definitions which are true for an infinite set, but which are only explicitly defined for a small subset. This is illustrated in the case of multiplication which we met above. Here the only explicit definition relates to how to multiply by one, and multiplication by any other positive integer is defined implicitly through the recursion.

The problem which we shall face in general in using these recursive definitions of functions and procedures is going to be how we can justify the statement that we have found a satisfactory realisation of a given specification. We would like to be able to show that our recursive definition gives an accurate realisation of the specification for every integer value of the parameters, but it is not immediately clear how we could do this, since we cannot check the definition for each of an infinite number of different cases. The principle of mathematical induction provides exactly the tool which we require.

6.8   Introducing the tool: Mathematical Induction

Let's imagine that we want to prove that something is true for every possible value of a particular positive integer. For example, speaking mathematically, we might want to show that the sum

$$1 + 2 + 3 + ... + n = n(n+1)/2$$

Mathematicians can prove this result using the principle of mathematical induction and the technique is fairly straightforward for us to master. Notice that the statement here has a parameter, n, whose value can be chosen as any positive whole number. The statement which we are aiming to prove is therefore a composite statement which encompasses separate statements for each of the possible values of $n = 1, 2, 3$, etc..

In other words, we need to show that

$$1 = 1(1+1)/2$$

$$1 + 2 = 2(2+1)/2$$

$$1 + 2 + 3 = 3(3+1)/2$$

and so on.

The recipe goes as follows:

1. We show that the statement is true for a particular fixed value of the parameter. Typically we choose the value n=1 to start the induction.

2. We assume the statement to be true for a fixed value of n(=r) and we show that it is then also true for n=r+1.

Having completed these two stages, we can conclude that the given statement is true for every possible value of n. (i.e. for n=1,2,3 etc.)

This overall conclusion is justified, since if the statement is true for n=1, which we will have proved in stage 1, then by stage 2 it will also be true for n=2. By repeatedly applying stage 2, we may then deduce that the statement is true for n=3,4,5 etc., and hence for all positive whole number values for n.

We can now apply this method to the statement above, to illustrate how a mathematician would use an inductive argument:

For convenience, we shall call the statement

$$1 + 2 + 3 + \ldots + n = n(n+1)/2$$

by the name P_n

Stage 1 of the proof now concerns showing P_1 is true. In other words, we need to show that

$$1 = 1(1+1)/2$$

This is clearly true, and we can therefore move on to considering the second stage of the induction.

For stage 2, we assume that P_r is true. In other words, we assume that

$$1 + 2 + \ldots + r = r(r+1)/2$$

and we need to show that P_{r+1} is true. P_{r+1} states that $1 + 2 + \ldots + r + r + 1 = (r+1)(r+2)/2$ If we take the left hand side of P_{r+1}, we have

$$P_{r+1} = 1 + 2 + \ldots + r + r + 1 = r(r+1)/2 + r + 1$$

by the assumption that P_r is true

$$P_{r+1} = r(r+1) + 2(r+1)/2 = (r+1)(r+2)/2$$

which demonstrates that the left hand side of P_{r+1} is the same as the right hand side of the statement, and hence the induction stage 2 is complete.

Therefore the proof is completed, and we may conclude that the statement P_n is proved true for every possible choice of positive integer n.

The method which we have discussed here will be applied to showing that a realisation which uses recursion is indeed satisfying a specification. The reader may find it helpful to try some simple mathematical applications of induction before attempting to apply the methods to examples expressed using VDM. Therefore the following exercises are offered by way of practice. However they may be omitted by those with a mathematical background, and readers who would prefer to work directly in software related applications.

6.9   Exercises

1. Prove that

$$1^2 + 2^2 + ... + n^2 = n(n+1)(2n+1)/6$$

   for every positive whole number n.

2. Prove that

$$1^3 + 2^3 + ... + n^3 = n^2(n+1)^2/4$$

   for every positive whole number n.

Note: Example solutions to these exercises are given in appendix I.

6.10   Recursive definitions, induction and VDM

We turn now to consider how a recursive definition of a function or procedure is shown to satisfy its specification, expressed using VDM.

To begin with, we consider again the multiplication function for two positive integers a and b.

We make the following specification in VDM:

Mult(a,b:Posint)c:Posint
    PRE: True
    POST: $c = a \times b$
and we aim to prove that
    Mult(a,b) if b = 1 then a else a + mult(a,b-1)
is a valid realisation of the specification.

We shall present the proof using the method of mathematical induction which we discussed in the previous section:

  1. $a \in Z^+$
  2. $b \in Z^+$
  3. mult(a,1) = a Post-mult(a,b)
  4. mult(a,b) = a × b Inductive hypothesis
  5. mult(a,b+1) = a + mult(a,b) Definition of mult()
  6. mult(a,b+1) = a + a × b Subs 4
  7. mult(a,b+1) = a × b+1
  8. Infer mult(a,b)= a × b N-induction

The lines numbered 1-3 in this proof correspond to the stage 1 of the previous description of inductive proofs, and lines 4-7 correspond to stage 2.

Having spent some time establishing a recursive definition which is simple (and fairly obvious), we shall now turn our attention to establishing satisfiability of a recursive definition for a function which is more worthwhile, complex and which has a data processing basis.

6.11   Example: The function Highestpaid

In a particular data processing program, which has a stored collection of employee names and their salary levels, we desire a function which will provide the name of the employee with the largest salary. In this section, we shall write down a VDM specification of this requirement, and a recursive definition of a suitable function.

A suitable specification is as follows:

> Highestpaid(set:employee-record-set)answer:employee-record
> > Pre: set $\neq$ {}
> > Post: { answer $\in$ set } $\land$
> > > { $\forall$ employee $\in$ set employee-salary $\leq$ answer-salary }

We shall define the function recursively. It will be convenient to introduce a parameter n, which identifies the size of the set.

Highestpaidn(set,n) if n=1 then first-record
> else Higherof(first-record, Highestpaidn(set - first-record,n-1))
> There are two particular points to notice here.

Firstly, we have required an additional function Higherof. This is a function which compares the salaries of two records and returns the record with the higher salary. We can specify this function easily, and a simple implementation can be proved. We give the specification and realisation explicitly, but leave the proof of satisfiability to the reader, since it is straightforward.

Secondly, we are assuming that it is possible to split a set up into the first record, and the remainder of the set. The implementation of this will be dependent upon suitable language statements being available in the selected implementation medium. (As usual, a programmed example is given in appendix I to illustrate how this example could be implemented in practice).

For the function Higherof, a suitable specification in VDM is as follows:

> Higherof(a,b:employee-record)c:employee-record
> > Pre: True
> > Post: $c \in \{a, b\}$, c-salary $\geq$ a-salary, c-salary $\geq$ b-salary

and a suitable realisation of the function would be:
> **Higherof(a,b)** if a-salary $>$ b-salary then a else b

We shall turn our attention next to the proof of satisfiability of the recursive definition of the function Highestpaid.

The specification was defined as

Highestpaid(set:employee-record-set)answer:employee-record
        Pre: set $\neq$ {}
        Post: { answer $\in$ set } $\wedge$
                { $\forall$ employee $\in$ set employee-salary $\leq$ answer-salary }

with the realisation
        Highestpaidn(set,n)
                if n=1 then first-record else
                        Higherof(first-record, Highestpaidn(set - first-record,n-1))

We prove the satisfiability of the realisation by induction.

1. Highestpaidn(set,1) = first-record
2. Post-Highestpaid(set, Highestpaidn(set,1))
3. Post-Highestpaid(set_n, Highestpaidn(set_n,n))
        Inductive hypothesis
4. Highestpaidn(set_{n+1},n+1) =
        Higherof(first-record, Highestpaidn(set_{n+1} - first-record))
        by realisation
5. Highestpaidn(set_{n+1},n+1) =
        Higherof(first-record, Highestpaidn(set_n,n)
        by properties of sets
6. Highestpaidn(set_{n+1},n+1) =
        Higherof(first-record, Highestpaid(set_n)
        by Inductive hypothesis
7. Highestpaidn(set_{n+1},n+1) $\geq$ first-record-salary
8. Highestpaidn(set_{n+1},n+1) $\geq$ Highestpaid(set_n)
9. Post-Highestpaid(set_{n+1},Highestpaidn(set_{n+1},n+1))

Notation:

Here we have used statements of the form

Post-Highestpaid(set_{n+1},Highestpaidn(set_{n+1},n+1)). This type of statement is used to make the point that Highestpaidn(set_{n+1},n+1) satisfies the post-condition for Highestpaid(set_{n+1})

This completes the proof by induction, and we are therefore able to conclude that the function Highestpaid which is realised here is a faithful realisation of the specification of the function given using VDM.

6.12   What happens when a realisation fails to meet the specification?

We have stated earlier in this book, that one of the principal motives for introducing formal techniques into the software specification process is to improve the quality of the software produced. This in turn will happen, only if the errors in implementation are highlighted by the development process. It is therefore reasonable to question what will happen if we have an inadequate or incorrect realisation of a specification, and we nevertheless attempt to prove it to be correct.

The simple answer to this question is that the proof will not work (or at least, if it does, then we must have made an error!) However, just because we are unable to prove something doesn't necessarily always mean that it is not true, and could not be proved by somebody else. Therefore, if we have reason to believe that a given realisation does not satisfy its specification, then the appropriate thing to do is to search for something called a *counterexample*.

A counterexample is an example which can be applied both to the specification and to the realisation and which gives different results in the two cases. The existence of these different results shows that the realisation cannot be equivalent to the original specification, since if they are equivalent then they are bound to produce the same results.

However, counterexamples are not always easy to find. One of the problems with software which is developed conventionally is that the testing process doesn't always find the appropriate data to use to test the software and to show up the errors which exist. In the same way, the search for a counterexample which will show a realisation to be inaccurate is sometimes long and difficult. On the positive side however, once a satisfiability proof is complete, there is no need to search for counterexamples, since the proof demonstrates that no such counterexamples can exist.

This indicates once again the advantage of the formal approach, since once the quite difficult problem of proving satisfiability is complete, there are no further questions to answer.

For the present, we shall consider a very straightforward example of an erroneous realisation. Consider again the example which we discussed earlier of multiplcation. We shall use the same specification, but an alternative realisation:

The specification which we are working from is therefore

Mult(a,b:Posint)c:Posint
        PRE: True
        POST: c= a × b
and we aim to prove that
        Mult(a,b) if b = 1 then a else b + mult(a,b-1)

is a valid realisation of the specification.

We can show that this realisation is invalid by choosing suitable numbers for a and b. For example, if a=3 and b=6, the Post-condition of the specification gives mult(3,6)=18, while the realisation gives:

Mult(3,6) = 6 + Mult(3,5)
        = 6 + 5 + Mult(3,4)
        = 6 + 5 + 4 + Mult(3,3)
        = 6 + 5 + 4 + 3 + Mult(3,2)
        = 6 + 5 + 4 + 3 + 2 + Mult(3,1)
        = 6 + 5 + 4 + 3 + 2 + 3
        = 23

Since $18 \neq 23$, the realisation does not satisfy the specification.

6.13   Exercises

1. Can you find two pairs of values of a and b for which the incorrect realisation of Mult(a,b) given above does agree with the specification? Note: This demonstrates the well known fact that to prove that a statement is true, it must be shown true in every possible case, and exhibiting an example is not sufficient proof, while to show a statement is false, we need only exhibit a single counterexample.

2. For each of the following VDM specifications, determine whether the given function is a faithful realisation of the specification. If the function is a true realisation of the specification, give a proof by induction that this is the case. Otherwise give a clear indication of where the given realisation fails to meet the specification. (If you require assistance then refer to appendix I).

   a. Specification:

   Addup(a: a $\in$ Z, a ¿ 0) = 1 + 2 + ... + a

   Realisation:

   If a=1 then Addup = 1 else Addup = Addup(a-1) + a

   b. Specification:

   Factorial(a: a $\in$ Z, a > 0) = 1 $\times$ 2 $\times$ 3 ... $\times$ a

   Realisation:

   Factorial = a $\times$ Factorial(a-1)

   c. Specification:

   Add2(a: a=2b, b $\in$ Z, b > 0) = 2 + 4 + ... + a

   Realisation:

   Add2 = a(a+2)/2

Chapter 7

Data Structures

7.1 Introduction

In this chapter, we shall begin to discuss data structures, and how they may be expressed using formal methods. We have already alluded to the data structures issue in the previous chapter, where we experienced some difficulty in considering lists of data items and needed to worry about whether the idea of a *list* indicated a particular type of implementation. In this chapter, we shall begin by discussing the *set*, which is a fundamental and simple data structure. We then consider how composite data structures may be formed from simple data structures such as sets. Finally, we consider how it may be possible, for some applications, to consider the data structure as being *external* to our current processing, and therefore to treat the data structure as a *black box*.

7.2 Background

When designing a computer system, we almost always are concerned with data. Modelling a system involves careful consideration of the data which needs to be stored, and how it should be accessed and processed. All this involves thinking about the *structure* of the data.

The structure which the data should display is, or should be, imposed by the problem which we are working on. There are also the constraints imposed by the machine, or the language which we are using to make an efficient implementation. This means the implementation needs to be designed to have the data structures conforming to the capabilities of the machine and the language being used.

Obviously, this last point will be important when we come to the implementation stage, but in common with our earlier practice within this book, we shall concern ourselves primarily with the desire to design a *specification* which matches the original problem as closely as possible. (See figure 7.1).

7.3   Sets

The fundamental data structure is the set. The concept of a set is familiar to those who have followed 'modern' mathematics syllabuses for some 30 years now, and is in any case a straightforward extension of our everyday understanding of the word.

In many ways, a set lacks 'structure' since it consists simply of a collection of objects. Any given object either belongs in the set or it doesn't.

We have already discussed several sets within this book. We have not bothered to call them sets, because we have assumed a common understanding with the reader of what the objects are. For example, we met the positive whole numbers. This is a set, because it is a collection of objects. If you were given any object, then you could determine whether the object you were given was in the set Z^+ of 'positive whole numbers' or not.

So, for example, the number 3 is in Z^+ while -4 is not in Z^+

and the object 'banana' is not in Z^+

When we were discussing the library system in the previous chapters, we were considering the borrowers from the library, and the books which they had borrowed. The borrowers belonging to the library form a set of people, which is a subset of the local population, and the books in the library form a set of books which is a subset of the set of all possible books in the world.

Therefore, the idea of a set is both simple and natural. It is not a complicated idea which is hard to follow, even though its roots lie in

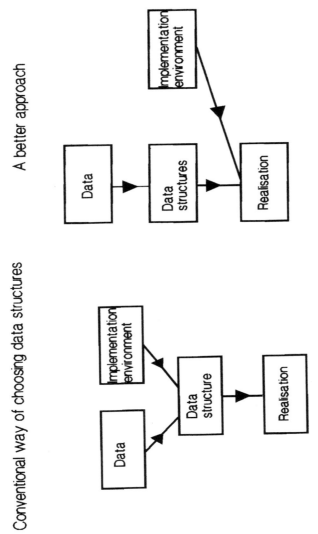

Figure 7.1 Data structures should be chosen firstly to implement the data requirements and only secondly to conform to the capabilities of the machine

abstract mathematics.

There are various things which we can do with sets. There are a series of natural questions which we can ask:

Assume S is a set, then we could ask the following questions:

1. Is the object x a member of the set S? i.e. is $x \in S$?

2. Is the set T a subset of the set S. i.e. is $T \subset S$? In other words, is every member of T also a member of S? We might write this down mathematically, the question we would be asking would be phrased as follows: $\forall t \in T, t \in S$; which is read as for every t in T, t is in S.

3. What are the elements common to the two sets S and T. In other words, we would be seeking their *intersection* $S \cap T$.

4. What are the elements which make up the union of the two sets S and T. We write this as $S \cup T$.

A common means of representing sets, widely used by mathematicians, is the Venn diagram. Several examples of Venn diagrams are shown in figure 7.2. Their principal feature is the desire to give a visual representation of the inter-relationships of sets with one another.

The sorts of questions which we listed above are the aspects of set theory which are most commonly discussed by mathematicians, but they are not necessarily the ones which we will find the most useful from a software specification viewpoint.

We shall consider here again an example which we have discussed before. In a bank computer system, there will be a program for dealing with the customers' accounts. So for example, the program will deal with holding the customers' names and addresses and details of their bank account numbers. What operations would we expect this program to deal with?

We can begin by thinking about what sort of information must be stored by a bank's computer system so that it can respond to all the demands which are made of it. We can then move on to consider the processing which will be needed. On reflection, it becomes clear that the information stored is a set of items of data, each relating to a single bank customer.

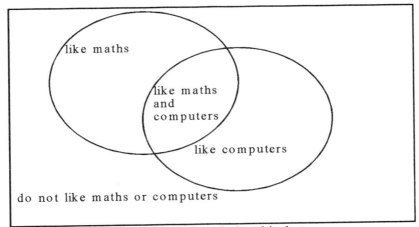

Venn diagram illustrating the relationship between
the students in a particular group who like
Mathematics and those who like Computer Science.

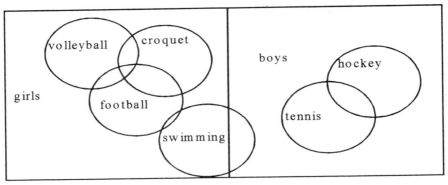

Venn diagram illustrating the relationship between
children in a particular class who do various sports.

Figure 7.2 Examples of Venn diagrams

We can identify the following list of processes which will certainly be required of the system:

1. A new customer joins the bank. The program must be able to add an extra object to the set of data objects stored.

2. A customer changes address or name. The program must be able to take the existing data item which relates to the customer and make amendments to it.

3. A customer leaves the bank, and the appropriate object must be removed from the set.

4. The bank wishes to send out a letter, and uses the program to check on whether the customer exists and to find the name and address.

If we consider these, very natural operations, we can see that they are just the sorts of operations which will be common to very many data processing applications of computers. The need to *maintain* a database is common to almost all modern applications, and maintenance of a database involves operations on the set of objects stored which allow us to add, delete, amend and lookup data items.

From the viewpoint of our set theory, therefore, we shall need the following operations:

1. Delete. We need to be able to make the original set lose the object x. i.e. $S \rightarrow S - \{x\}$

2. Insert. We need to be able to produce a set which has all the original members and one additional member. ie $S \rightarrow S + \{x\}$.

3. Amend. We need to be able to replace an existing member of the set by a changed version. i.e. $S \rightarrow S - \{x\} + \{x'\}$

4. Locate. We need to be able to find a particular element in S. In other words, we are seeking an element x in S which satisfies some property, y, say. i.e. $\exists x \in S|y$.

7.4   How can we use sets?

The previous example gives some indication of the sort of situation where a set may be useful. When there is some underlying set from which the particular items which we are interested in are drawn, it makes sense to describe the underlying data-set as a set! The fundamental property of a set is that it comes with no prescribed ordering of the elements- they may appear in any order, and there is no clear indication that one should naturally come before another.

This property of sets can mean that in practical applications, they are less useful than they might be. Later in this chapter we discuss some alternative data structures in which there is a natural order and which can therefore be manipulated in some simple and natural ways. If data is stored in a set, the absence of any prescribed order means that processing cannot be performed in a logical order. So, for example, it is difficult to perform an operation to each element in a set, since one has no option of starting at the beginning and working through one by one.

From our point of view, the direct result of this is that it can be rather difficult to complete proofs of specifications and realisations which involve sets, since there is no natural mathematical tool which can work through such an unstructured entity in a logical and rigorous way. The solution which is adopted is either

1. To undertake the proof by exhaustion (i.e. by considering each element of the set in turn, and having shown exhaustively the result for every possibility we may then deduce that the result is always true.

   or

2. To proceed with a proof by induction, where the inductive hypothesis takes as its parameter the size n of the underlying set.

We can see the latter approach used in the previous chapter where we showed how a method can be employed to sort items into order, and the method works by assuming an existing method for sorting smaller sets, and showing that the problem is simple for a set of just one item.

7.5   Data processing and data structures

One of the arguments which is propounded by software engineers and others in the software development process is that examining the structure of data is at least as important as examining the processing which is to be undertaken. Therefore, it is argued, the primary consideration should be to think about how the data is to be structured and stored within the system rather than to begin by considering what processing will be required.

To some extent, this argument is correct. Simply storing data in a form which will lead to ease of processing but which loses the fundamental properties and structure of the data being stored is ill-advised. On the other hand, storing data in the most natural way, without considering how it should be processed and what constraints the method of storage might be placing upon the subsequent processing is equally inappropriate.

The **set** is the most *natural* way to store typical unordered collections of data items, but it is not often the most convenient from a processing point of view, as we have just seen. Therefore it can often be advisable to collect data and store it with some *additional structure* above its *natural structure* to ease processing.

In the next sections, we shall see how *composite* data types can be constructed to allow for the storage of data in a flexible way, and to permit the introduction of additional structure which will assist in the processing (and in the provability of the specifications which are realised in an implementation).

7.6   Composite objects

Experienced programmers will realise that applications rarely use data objects which are *simple*. Most data processing involves manipulating data which is held in records. For example, in a computerised library system, each borrower record would contain *fields* relating to the name, address, borrower number and probably various other information. On the other hand, the book record contains details such as the title, author, publisher, date of publication and price.

These data items, are *composite objects*. By a composite object, we shall mean an object which is made up of simple objects, joined together, and each simple object is associated with particular aspects of the item to which it refers.

In order to illustrate this more clearly, we can think about the date: Today is Tuesday 14th April 1992.

This date is made up of four simple objects.

- Tuesday

- 14th

- April

- 1992

We could specify this composite data structure for a date, which we shall call **fulldate**, in the following way using VDM:

compose Fulldate of

Dayname : $\{1, ..., 7\}$,

Daynumber : $\{1, ..., 31\}$,

Monthnumber : $\{1, ..., 12\}$,

Yearnumber : N

end

and we require a *make function* for Fulldate would then be defined by the mapping mk-Fulldate:

mk-Fulldate:$\{1, ..., 7\} \times \{1, ..., 31\} \times \{1, ..., 12\} \times N$

Today's date would then be recorded as

mk-Fulldate(3,14,4,1992)

The mapping mk-Fulldate, known as a *make* function, is used to map the particular values for the Dayname, Daynumber, Monthnumber, and Yearnumber into the corresponding composite object Fulldate. These make functions are sometimes known as *constructors*, since they are used to construct new data types. (Figures 7.3 and 7.4).

The inverse of a constructor is a *selector*. Corresponding to the Fulldate definition given here, we could define four selectors. These selectors would, respectively, return the values of the Day's name (1=Sunday, 2=Monday etc), Day number (i.e. 1st to 31st), Month number

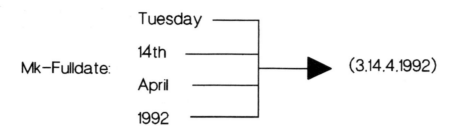

Figure 7.3 The make function, Mk-Fulldate, maps four simple objects to an abstract composite object.

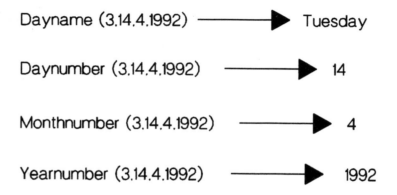

Figure 7.4 The selectors, Dayname, Daynumber, Monthnumber, and Yearnumber each map the composite abstract data object to a simple object.

(1-12) and Year number. It would be convenient to call them by the identifiers Dayname, Daynumber, Monthnumber and Yearnumber.

We would then have Dayname(mk-Fulldate(3,14,4,1992))=3 etc..

Notice the specifications of these last functions, since

Dayname : Fulldate → 1,...,7,

Daynumber : Fulldate → 1,...,31,

Monthnumber : Fulldate → 1,...,12

and

Yearnumber : Fulldate → N.

Notice how the compose...end construction corresponds to the method of defining data types in some high level languages. This close correspondence will make it relatively easy for us to prove the equivalence of the program statements when the specification is written in this form.

For example, in Pascal, we cound write the type declaration for Fulldate in the following form:

type Fulldate =

record

Daynumber : 1..31;

Monthnumber : 1..12;

Yearnumber : integer

end;

7.7 Exercises

1. Rewrite the **compose** expression for Fulldate in a high level language of your choice.

2. Sketch the contents of a typical record in a library system borrower database. Determine the fields needed and their sizes and types. Then write the compose statement using VDM, and a suitable make function. Convert your VDM version of **compose** into a suitable declaration in Pascal or some other suitable high level language.

7.8 Problems arising in specifications of data structures

If we consider the definition of Fulldate given previously, we have
    compose Fulldate of
Dayname : $\{1, ..., 7\}$,
Daynumber : $\{1, ..., 31\}$,
Monthnumber : $\{1, ..., 12\}$,
Yearnumber : N
    end

Thus we could, from this definition of Fulldate, take any Dayname from 1 to 7 with any Daynumber from 1 to 31, any Monthnumber from 1 to 12 and any Yearnumber. In practice, many of these combinations will be unacceptable. For example choosing Daynumber=31 and Monthnumber=2 will give the 31st of February. Therefore we should really give more information in the specification.

As becomes clear very quickly, there is an enormous amount of such additional information to be given in order to complete this definition, because not only do the Daynumbers depend upon the Monthnumbers and, in the case of February, upon the Yearnumbers, but also the Daynames depend upon a complicated inter-relationship between all three other fields.

All this illustrates that consistency checking becomes extremely difficult, and giving a full specification can be very complex. For the purposes of this book, we will not go into further detail in this area, but refer the reader to Jones (1990).

7.9 Keeping data abstract and implicit

One of the features of formal methods which we have identified previously is the desire to maintain an abstract, implicit, and implementation free approach to our work. One of the dangers when we fail to do this is that we can spend too much time and effort worrying about how we are going to manage to do something. This can mean that we never really get a clear idea of what exactly it is that we are trying to do!

The consideration of data structures is a case in point. Previously in this chapter, we discussed the merits of working on the structure of data independently of the processing which was to be undertaken. This approach has some advantages, but also has the danger that the data structures will be inappropriate for some necessary processing.

For example, a computerised hospital admissions system could hold a waiting list of patients. These names would naturally be held in an ordered list. A second list could be held of the patients on the waiting list who have been admitted or given appointments. This situation is illustrated in figure 7.5.

A natural way of storing the data to reflect its underlying structure would be to use a linked list (as shown in figure 7.6. This list allows for the data items to be stored one after another, and retrieved in order whenever necessary. Therefore the data structure reflects accurately the data which we are storing.

One feature of the processing of this system will be the need to cancel appointments because of staff illness and unavailability of beds. In this case, there will be a need to find the last entry on the admissions list since this is the one which should be postponed. Clearly this can be done using the structure shown in figure 7.6, but a doubly linked list (figure 7.7) would make processing more straightforward.

On the other hand, it is sometimes appropriate to consider the processing requirements without worrying at all about the data structures. This is indeed natural in many instances where we are considering a particular feature of a problem and wish to present a description of the processing which needs to go on in this particular part of the solution without thinking at all about what happens elsewhere.

For example, if we consider the library computer system which we have described at several points already. Naturally there will be a database which contains the names and addresses of the borrowers. One of the operations which the computer system must undertake is to be able to maintain this database.

Now we could obviously describe the process of updating the database in terms of a detailed description of the existing database and the form of its content. However this would be both inappropriate and unnatural.

What we should do is to describe the database as if it was a 'black

Waiting list	Appointment/admission list		
patient1	patient1	appointment	12/4/1994
patient2	patient2	admitted	3/7/1993
patient3	patient3	admitted	7/6/1993
patient4	patient4	appointment	3/5/1994
patient5	patient6	admitted	3/6/1993
patient6	patient9	admitted	7/7/1993
patient7	.		
patient8	.		
patient9	.		

.
.
.

Figure 7.5 A hospital might wish to keep two lists of patients: a waiting list of patients requiring treatment and a list of those patients who have been given appointments or admitted to hospital.

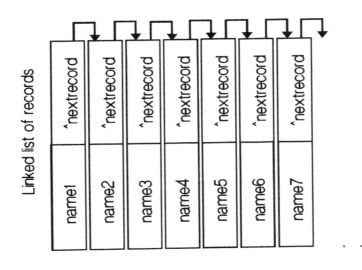

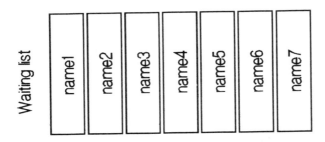

Figure 7.6 A linked list could be used to store a sequence of records containing information about patients on a waiting list.

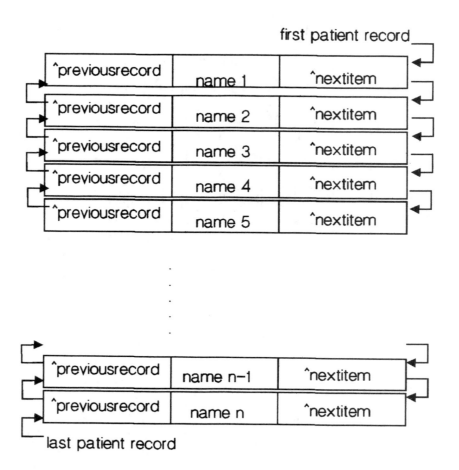

Figure 7.7 A doubly-linked list enables records to be located easily either from the top or bottom of the list.

box'. We do not really need to know how it is organised, nor exactly what the record structure is. Instead, we can consider the database simply as a set of records where each of the records corresponds to a single borrower.

The problem of maintaining the database is now reduced to the standard tasks which were identified earlier in the present chapter. These were:

adding an item
deleting an item
amending an item.

Considered as a 'black box' set of records, we are able to give a very clear description of these procedures. In doing this, we shall use the 'external' feature of VDM. The external feature allows us to describe how what we are doing influences something which is defined and used outside the current procedure or function.

ADDENTRY(p:Person)
ext wr database:Person-set
database = database $\cup \{p\}$ DELETEENTRY(p:Person)

ext wr database:Person-set
database = database $- \{p\}$ AMENDENTRY(p,p':Person)

ext wr database:Person-set
database = database $- \{p\} \cup \{p'\}$

Note: Here each of the external uses of **database** specifies that the contents of the external database may be changed (written to = wr). In some instances, an external value may be needed only for reference and not for amending and it is then referred to as ext rd.

The use of external items in the above specification has several advantages. The one which applies in the present discussion is that we are not influencing work which is done elsewhere on the same borrower database. This is appropriate, since, as we have already identified, the work done in updating the database is routine and should not influence any of the other aspects of the system. (Figure 7.8).

But there are other reasons for using external facilities. External variables may be used in place of parameters in definitions of functions

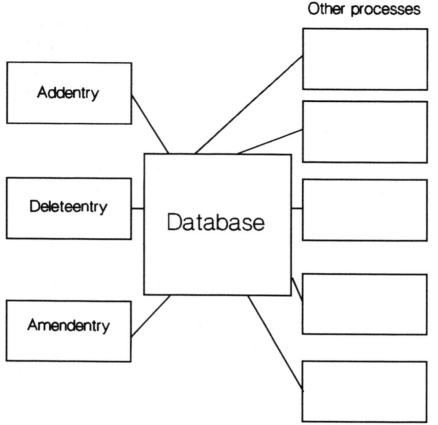

Figure 7.8 A database may be acted on by various processes. It can be thought of as external to each of the processes.

or procedures. They can also be used to return the values (answers) from a computed function or procedure. The advantages of using external variables rather than parameters only really becomes clear in specific examples, and some suitable simple examples are given below.

7.10   Examples

1. Specification of a process to compute the sum of the first n whole numbers:

   ADDUP

   Ext wr n, wr s_n

   Post $s_n = 1 + 2 + ... + n$

   Implementation

   $s_n = 1$

   while $n > 1$ do

   begin

   $s_n = s_n + n$

   $n = n - 1$

   end.

   Notice that no value for n is specified in the POST condition, and that the value of n at the end of the process may therefore vary in different implementations.

2. If we consider again the question of the bank account computer system, we can specify the processes which:

   - Output the current balance for a given account holder

     Ext rd Accountdatabase: set of account records, rd Accountnumber: number, wr Accountdetails: account record

     POST (Accountdetails.Accountnumber = Accountnumber) $\wedge$ (Accountdetails $\in$ Accountdatabase) $\wedge$ (Output balance)

- Update the database after a new account record has been made, and replace the old record.

  Ext wr Accountdatabase: set of account records, rd Oldaccountdetails , Newaccountdetails: account record

  PRE (Oldaccountdetails $\in$ Accountdatabase)

  POST Accountdatabase = Accountdatabase - {Oldaccountdetails $\cup$ {Newaccountdetails}

7.11   Exercises

1. Specify a process to calculate the sum of the first n square numbers

$$1^2 + 2^2 + ... + n^2$$

2. Specify a process to produce a list of all the bank account numbers held by Fred Smith.

3. Specify a number of processes to deal with borrowing books from and returning books to a public library.

Chapter 8

Some data processing

8.1   Introduction

In this chapter, we shall give some thought to issues relating to data processing. As a result, we shall be led to consider the concept of a *mapping* as a natural part of a data processing design. We shall then go on to consider the concept of a *sequence*, which also arises naturally in many data processing examples.

8.2   Background

In a data processing problem, we are typically storing, accessing and updating a *database* or *file* of information which is used as the basis for making some sorts of decision. Thus, a payroll program is designed to store details of the employee's tax and national insurance position together with details about pay scales, and the decision made is to determine the amount of pay due in a given period. Similarly a stock control system would store details of the catalogue numbers of stock items and their current stock levels; would update the data stored to take account of deliveries and sales, and would decide on the list of items which should be re-ordered.

8.3   The library system

The library system which we have described throughout this book needs to hold two lots of data. One will refer to the borrowers, their names and addresses and how many books they are allowed to borrow. The second database stores details about the books, their titles and authors, their publishers, their classification numbers and whether they are currently on loan. If a book is on loan, then details stored record to whom, and when it is due for return. The decisions made by this system will include

- who to send reminders to about overdue books

- which books are in great demand which justifies ordering additional copies

and so on.

Thus, in each case, decisions are made which are based upon information already to hand, and which result in one of a range of outcomes.

To take a simple example first, consider the library computer system and that part of it which issues reminders about overdue books. We can think of the possible *outcomes* from this part of the system. For each borrower, there are two possible outcomes:

1. Send a reminder about overdue books
2. Do not send a reminder about overdue books.

These two outcomes represent the entire set of possibilities, and for each member of the library, a decision will have to be made as to which outcome is appropriate.

Describing this in mathematical terms (and using the notation of VDM) this simply means we identify the *co- domain* as being the set of outcomes possible. In other words, the co-domain is the set { Send a reminder, Don't send a reminder}. The *domain* is then the set of all possible objects to which the decision has to be applied.

In the current example, it is evident that the domain is the set of all members of the library. The decision making process then defines a *mapping* or a *function* from the domain into the co-domain. We shall consider the distinction made between mappings and functions in the next section.

We shall call the mapping (function) *Whethertoremind* and we can make the following initial specification:

Whethertoremind :

$\{x \ : \ x$ is a library member $\} \ \rightarrow \ \{$Send a reminder, Don't send a reminder$\}$.

A mapping will define an *explicit* rule which shows how particular elements of the left hand set are associated with elements of the right hand set. We may surmise at this stage that the rule will have something to do with the question of how many books have been borrowed and how much overdue they are, but from our formal method viewpoint, for the time being we have simply identified that such a rule is to exist.

8.4   Mappings or functions?

So, what is different about mappings when compared with the functions which we have met previously? When we meet a function, we would usually have some sort of calculation to undertake in order to find the answer. If we consider the previous discussion, the payroll example describes the sort of application where a function would be appropriate. To calculate the pay due to an employee would involve multiplying the hourly rate by the number of hours worked, deducting tax and national insurance contributions and finishing with the value of the payment to be made. This is a common sort of calculation which uses some sort of formula.

On the other hand, many data processing applications involve something much more simple which is better described using the case-by-case explicit representation which we shall insist on for a map.

Thus, a mapping lists *every possible value* from the domain in turn, and associates with it explicitly a value from the co-domain. So, for example, a mapping could be set up to indicate on which floor in a library a particular type of book is stored. We could have the mapping *Whichfloor*

Whichfloor = { Sciencefiction $\rightarrow$ 1, Romance $\rightarrow$ 1, Historical $\rightarrow$ 2, Crime $\rightarrow$ 3, Non-fiction $\rightarrow$ Ground } which defines a mapping from the domain { Sciencefiction, Romance, Historical, Crime, Non-fiction } to the co-domain { Ground, 1, 2, 3 }.

In this last case, it is clear that it would be inappropriate for a function to be attempted. The simplest way to specify what it is that we require is to list all the possibilities, and no suitable *calculation* would be possible.

For the overdue books example, the question of whether to define a function or a mapping is rather more complicated: some people would find it easier to define a function which used a calculation something like this:

if borrower has books totalling more than 20 days overdue then send a reminder

This would clearly be a function, since it involves a calculation upon which the decision depends.

Alternatively, with the details of books borrowed stored alongside the book description it could be argued that a mapping from the date a book is due to be returned to the co-domain
{ Send a reminder, Don't send a reminder }
could be defined as

    { 10th April → Send a reminder,
    11th April → Send a reminder,
    12th April → Send a reminder,
    13th April → Send a reminder,
    14th April → Send a reminder,
    15th April → Send a reminder,
    16th April → Send a reminder,
    17th April → Don't send a reminder,
    18th April → Don't send a reminder,
    19th April → Don't send a reminder,
    20th April → Don't send a reminder,
    21st April → Don't send a reminder }
and so on.

Which approach would be more appropriate could vary. In practice, for this particular example, a manual system would probably approach the problem by means of a mapping, while an automated system would be more likely to use a function.

8.4.1   Exercise.

Why do you think that, for the library books reminder system, *a manual system would probably approach the problem by means of a mapping, while an automated system would be more likely to use a function?*

So, a mapping is more explicit than a function, and lists a finite set of outcomes. The mapping is applied by table look up methods to determine its effect on particular data items.

8.5   Manipulating Maps

Having determined a particular mapping, then what changes can we make to it? Interestingly, mappings are best thought of as a set of individual *maps* from one element of the domain to a single corresponding element of the co-domain. Therefore the range of operations which may be applied to a mapping is comparable to the range of operations which may be applied to a set.

In particular, we can identify the following:

8.5.1   Insertion of an additional map.

In the library book example which we discussed earlier, we have not defined any outcome corresponding to the date 22nd April. Therefore we might need to insert the additional map

22nd April → Don't send a reminder

into our mapping. We need to have a special notation to represent these insertions, and we use the symbol ⊙. The situation can arise where the attempted insertion of a map leads to a problem. This might happen if the inserted map leads to more than one image being defined for a given element in the domain. Where this is the case, the *outer* map is the one which is included in the final mapping. This is illustrated in the following example:

8.5.2   Example

With domain a,b,c,d,e and co-domain 1,2,3 we can define a mapping
Examplemap by
Examplemap = { a → 1, b → 2, c → 3 }
We can then use the insertion operation ⊙ as follows:
{ d → 1 } ⊙ Examplemap = { a → 1, b → 2, c → 3, d → 1 }
whereas
{ b → 1 } ⊙ Examplemap = { a → 1, b → 1, c → 3 }

8.5.3   Deletion of a map.

Again, this can be related to the library system, since once all books
due to be returned on a particular date have been returned, one of the
maps can be removed.

8.5.4   Unions and Intersections

If we have two mappings, we may take their set-wise union and their
set-wise intersection. In the case of the intersection, we are bound to
finish up with a new mapping; in the case of the union, we might finish
up with an invalid mapping, since we may have more than one image
for some elements of the domain.

For a specific example, consider the mappings:
Examplemap = { a → 1, b → 1, c → 3 }
and
Anothermap = { a → 1, b → 2, c → 3, d → 1, e → 1, f → 3 }
Then the set-wise union
Examplemap ∪ Anothermap = { a → 1, b → 1, c → 3, b → 2, d → 1,
e → 1, f → 3 }
contains the conflicting maps b → 1 and b → 2
while the intersection
Examplemap ∩ Anothermap = { a → 1, c → 3 }
is a mapping.

As can be seen from this example, we will need to apply some modified version of the insertion operation ⊙, in place of the set-wise union,

which can overcome this potential difficulty by prescribing which of the maps is retained when such a conflict arises.

8.6   Induction for mappings.

Inductive proofs were seen in our earlier discussion to be a powerful tool. If we wish to prove a proposition P_n is true for all values of the parameter n, then we proceed as follows:

1. We show that P_1 is true.

2. We assume that P_n is true for some value of n and show that P_{n+1} is also true.

We may then deduce that P_r is true for every positive whole number r.

   Sometimes we shall need to prove results for mappings, and here too some of the most significant results are proved by induction. The inductive method in this case is different. Jones (1990) gives the following representation of the induction for mappings:

$$p(\{\}); \quad \frac{d \in D, r \in R, m \in (D \to R), p(m), d \notin dom\, m \vdash p(\{d \mapsto r\} \odot m)}{m \in (D \to R) \vdash p(m)}.$$

We may well find it more convenient to express this as a step by step *recipe* for proving results about mappings inductively.

1. Express the proposition which we are trying to prove as a proposition of a mapping m, $p(m)$

2. Prove that $p(\{\})$ is true

3. Assume that $p(m)$ is true and let $\{d \mapsto r\}$ be a new map from the domain of m to its range, chosen so that d does not conflict with any existing domain elements which feature in the mapping m.

4. Prove that p is true when applied as $p(\{d \mapsto r\} \odot m)$.

8.7   Exercise:

Which of the following problems would most naturally be specified using a mapping, and which should use a function?

1. The prices of theatre tickets.

2. The amount of income tax payable by an individual.

3. The motor insurance premiums for different types of car.

8.8   Implementation of mappings

When a function is implemented, there is a rule which is applied to each input value from the domain in order to generate the value from the range which is appropriate. When we are dealing with mappings, on the other hand, it becomes necessary to use a more long-winded approach, based upon the idea of looking up the result in a table.

One way in which this can be achieved, is through the use of a *case* statement in a language such as Pascal. We can illustrate this for the type of simple example given above:

Let the mapping Examplemap be defined as follows:

Examplemap $= \{a \rightarrow 1, b \rightarrow 2, c \rightarrow 3\}$

then we can produce the required output from the following Pascal statement:

```
case domainelement of
a: examplemap:=1;
b: examplemap:=2;
c: examplemap:=3;
end;
```

8.9   Example

We have just described a Pascal case statement as being a method of implementing a mapping. In other words, we have claimed that the Pascal case statement satisfies the specification of a mapping. We shall now proceed to *prove* that this is indeed true.

Our proof proceeds by induction, and we follow the step-by-step guide which was given in 8.6.

Let m be a mapping and construct the Pascal case statement:

case domainelement of

    d_i: examplemap $:= r_i$

    end;

where the cases listed correspond to the maps $\{d_i \rightarrow r_i\} \in m$.

The statement $p(m)$ is formulated thus:

$p(m)$: **the case statement satisfies the specification of the mapping m.**

$p\{\}$ is clearly true since there is nothing to prove for an empty mapping.

Assume that $p(m)$ is true and let $\{d \rightarrow r\}$ be an additional map. Then

case domainelement of

    d_1: examplemap $:= r_1$;

    d_2: examplemap $:= r_2$;

    d_3: examplemap $:= r_3$;

    $\vdots$

    d_j: examplemap $:= r_j$

    end;

satisfies the specification for the mapping m, by the hypothesis $p(m)$ and we want to prove that

case domainelement of

    d_1: examplemap $:= r_1$;

    d_2: examplemap $:= r_2$;

    d_3: examplemap $:= r_3$;

    $\vdots$

    d_j: examplemap $:= r_j$

    d: examplemap $:= r$

    end;

satisfies the specification for the mapping $m \odot \{d \rightarrow r\}$.

We can show this last fact by observing that for every map in m, the case statement satisfies its specification (by $p(m)$) and for $\{d \rightarrow r\}$ the case statement satisfies its specification.

Hence the case statement satisfies the specification of the mapping $m \odot \{d \to r\}$ and $p(m \odot \{d \to r\})$ is true.

The induction is therefore completed and we have proved that $p(m)$ is true for all mappings m.

8.10   Exercise

Investigate how house contents insurance premiums are assessed by insurance companies. You will probably find some who use a function to calculate the premium and others who use a mapping. For one which uses a mapping, try to write a computer program which calculates house contents premiums.

8.11   Partitions and equivalence relations

One of the processes which is used repeatedly in computer programs, sometimes more explicitly than others, is the process of constructing a *partition*. By a partition, we simply mean splitting up the domain of a mapping into several subsets.

This constructing of a partition happens every time we make a decision. In the library book reminder example which we discussed earlier in this chapter, we constructed a partition of the possible dates when library books could be due for return into two sets. One of the sets was the dates due for which a reminder should be issued, and the other set was the set of dates due back for which no reminder need be sent yet.

So, the notion of constructing a partition is not new, even if the term *partition* is new. Whenever we construct a partition in this sort of context we are doing the following:

1. Associating together all those items for which the action to be taken should be the same.

2. Constructing a set of subsets of the domain which is

   - Exhaustive (i.e. every element in the domain appears in a subset)

- Disjoint (i.e. no element from the domain appears in more than one subset).

The number of different subsets in the partition can be large or small, according to the application. However, the important thing to remember is that every mapping and every decision which is taken implies the construction of a partition. A mapping defines a partition of its domain by collecting as the subsets those elements of the domain which map to each of the elements of the co-domain. (See figure 8.1).

Mathematicians often talk about the notion of an equivalence relation. All that is meant by an equivalence relation is a means of recognising those elements of a domain which have a common property. In data processing examples, we shall be constructing lots of relationships which could be shown to be equivalence relations, but they will all be of a common form. Two elements will have the common property (will *relate* or *be equivalent* to each other) if they both map to the same element of the co-domain, or if they both result in the same decision. Mathematicians prove, as we have observed, that each equivalence relation defines a partition of the domain.

8.12   Sequences

Data processing examples usually require the storage of large quantities of data, often in the form of records in a data structure of some sort, and one of the big issues which Computer Scientists must determine is how the data should be stored.

We have already discussed the ideas of sets, which are really rather unstructured data structures, since they describe a collection of data items which are either present or absent but have otherwise no inter-relationship. We have also considered the idea that data items are grouped, by means of some sort of partition or mapping into subsets.

It is natural for us to consider next the idea of storing the items in a particular sequence or order. This is a very natural way of considering data, and we have found it hard at times to avoid making the assumption that we could impose an order on the data. This is because it is far more usual to store and process data in *sequence* than in an

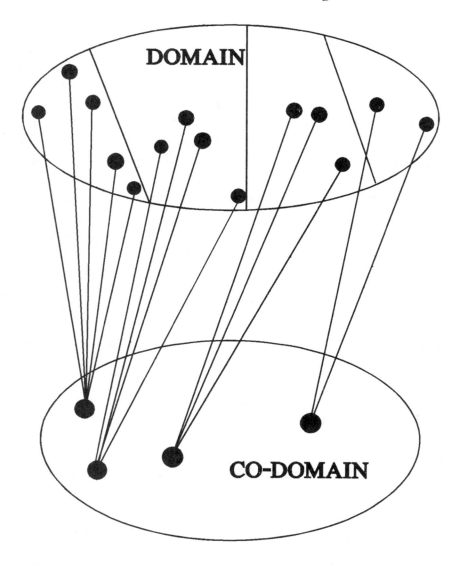

Figure 8.1 A mapping defines a partition of its domain

unstructured way.

Whenever we talk about a *list* of data items we are making precisely this assumption, since a list begins with one item and then each item follows in sequence, and so on. There are also, as those who have studied data structures previously will be aware, a whole variety of other similar data structures which are defined according to particular methods of construction and access, but which provide a fundamentally sequential method of storing data: these are the **stack**, the **queue**, and the **priority queue.**

The idea of sequential storage and processing of data is very natural. Nevertheless, when it comes to the definition of a sequence, and the operation of specifying and proving specifications, life becomes more complicated. This is because it is precisely those features of the sequence which give us the power to use the sequence more efficiently which add to the difficulty of its definition.

Take, for example, the idea of a list. We wish to write a specification of exactly what it means to have a list of data items, and we need to talk about how to manipulate the list to cope with keeping the data stored up to date.

To begin with, we will need a data item which is defined as the sort of thing which will be held in the list. We have seen in the previous chapter how we might construct a composite data item for this sort of purpose, and we assume for present purposes that this has been done, and that the resulting type is called *element*.

To define the list, we start by saying that the list consists of one element after another. We use an asterisk * to denote repetition:
element*

So far, we have simply made the statement that a list consists of one data object after another, which is a start! We now need to think about what is involved in undertaking the fundamental updating operations of insertion and deletion of elements from the list.

To insert an element, we need to form a list which agrees with the original list elements and has the additional new element added at the end. We can write this as a procedure specification as follows:
Addtolist(new:element)
    ext wr : currentlist:list
    post currentlist = $\overrightarrow{currentlist}$ [new]

Thus, we are specifying that currentlist should be made up of the old currentlist (denoted by *currentlist*) followed by the additional entry.

The process of removing an entry from the list is much more interesting and illustrates a number of the features of formal methods which we have identified earlier in this book. The difficulty which arises stems from the fact that we cannot tell where in the list an entry which is to be deleted lies. Therefore, when we delete an entry from the list, what we must do is to take the existing list, split it into two partlists, in order to remove the entry in question, and then rejoin the parts (see figure (8.2))

We can write this as follows:

Remove(old:element)
    ext wr currentlist:list
pre old $\in$ currentlist
post currentlist $=$
    firstpart$^\frown$secondpart
    $\wedge currentlist = $ firstpart$^\frown$[old]$^\frown$secondpart

Notice how this last specification displays all the features of implicitness which we have identified as being desirable. All we have said is that before we remove the item **old**, there was a sublist before it and a sublist after it. Now we are just left with the two sublists, concatenated (joined) to produce the whole list. The specification makes no attempt to demonstrate how we might go about implementing this in a programming language.

In fact, as we can see in the example which follows, this implicitness is essential in the current example, since some programming languages offer specific list processing facilities which require a very different approach from the one which would be needed in a more conventional high level language. Therefore any discussion of how exactly we might go about forming the necessary partition of the original list and locating the desired element for deletion could be misleading and counterproductive. (See figures 8.3 and 8.4).

1: Identify entry to be deleted

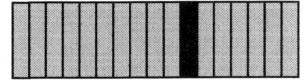

2: Split list into two partlists

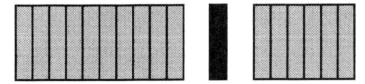

3: Rejoin the parts

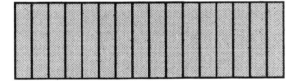

Figure 8.2 Steps involved in deleting an entry from a list

Prolog language statements to delete an element from a list.

We assume that we have a list called L1 and we wish to delete (the first occurence of) an element X from L1. We shall construct a rule of the form *delete(X,L1,L2)* which returns the list after removing X from L1 as the list L2.

delete(_,[ ],[ ]).
delete(A,[A|L],L) :- !.
delete(A,[B|L],[B|M]) :- delete(A,L,M).

The goal is *delete(X,L1,L2).*

Notice how the clauses are constructed.
- The first clause gives the information that when we delete anything from the empty list we finish up with nothing.
- The second clause says that if we start with a list that begins with an element, then we can delete the element simply by writing down the remaining elements of the original list.
- The third clause indicates that if the list begins with an element other than the element which we want to delete, then we simply strip off that element and repeat with the sublist.
- An inductive argument leads to a proof that this method is equivalent to that illustrated in figure 8.2.

Figure 8.3

This procedure is written in Turbo Pascal. We assume that a constant, ListSize, has been declared giving the maximum size of the list, and that the following type declaration has been made:

    ListType = array[1..ListSize] of string;

This procedure has as parameters the name to be deleted (X) and the array containing the list (L1). The resulting new list is returned in a variable parameter (L2). A special string element, '??????????', is used to indicate when the end of the list is reached.

```
procedure Delete(X:string; L1:ListType; var L2:ListType);
var
  i:integer;
begin
{A}
i := 1;                          {start at first name in list}
while (X <> L1[i])               {name not found}
    and (L1[i] <> '??????????') {end of list not reached}
do begin
  L2[i] := L1[i];                {copy to new list}
  i := i + 1;                    {go on to next name in list}
  end;
```

Figure 8.4 (Continued on next page)

```
{B}
while (L1[i] <> '??????????') do  {end of list not reached}
    begin
    L2[i] := L1[i+1];
    i := i+1;
    end;

{C}
L2[i] := '??????????';          {put end-of-list marker}
end;
```

The procedure falls into three parts:
Part A searches for the first occurrence of the string to be deleted. Note that the possibility of reaching the end of the list without finding the required string must be taken into account.
PartB effectively removes the required element from the list by 'moving up' each element of the list which occurs beyond it.
Part C marks the new end of the list.

Figure 8.4

8.13   Exercises

1. The queue is a data structure which allows for additional entries
   to be added to the rear of the queue and items to be removed only
   from the head of the queue. Write specifications for the queue
   itself, for a procedure to add an additional entry to the queue,
   and a procedure to remove the front entry from the queue.

2. The stack is a *last in first out* sequential data structure. This
   means that data items are added and removed from the same end
   of the stack. Write a specification for the stack, for the procedure
   push which adds an additional entry to the stack and for the
   procedure *pop* for removing an entry.

8.14   Why are sequences more complicated than sets and mappings?

From the above example, we may observe that, by comparison with sets
and maps, sequences are more complicated for two principal reasons:

1. The order of the items in the sequence is significant. This means
   that the order in which things are done becomes important. If we
   add an additional entry to a set or to a mapping, then whether
   we add on the left or the right is immaterial. This is not the
   case when we have any type of sequential storage. The sequence
   [a,b,c,d] is different from the sequence [b,c,d,a].

2. The items in a sequence may be repeated. We have previously
   seen that items within a set cannot be repeated. The elements
   of a set either belong or not, and we cannot have two or three
   or more copies of a particular element within the set. Similarly,
   with mappings, we have insisted that there is at most one map
   which takes a particular element of the domain into an element
   of the co-domain. We may not have a second element of the
   co-domain associated with the same element of the domain, and
   if any attempt is made to have this occur then we have rules
   prescribed for determining which of the two maps is included in

the final version. However, with a sequence, the same element may be repeated at will.

8.15   Operations on sequences

Apart from the usual operations of adding and deleting elements from a sequence, there are a number of further operations which apply to sequences and are rather different from corresponding operations, where they exist, for sets of other simpler structures.

1. Concatenation. Given two sequences S and T, we may form a new sequence which consists of the elements of S, followed by the elements of T. This operation is easier than the corresponding union of sets or of maps, because we do not need to worry about whether or not particular elements have been repeated in the case of concatenation of sequences.

2. Selection of the first or last element. Order of sets and maps is not defined, but for sequences the elements are in a clearly defined order. Indeed our discussions of lists, queues and stacks earlier made clear the way in which the orders of elements in sequences may be used to determine alternative methods of accessing data from within these structures. It would be meaningless to ask for the first or last element in a mapping or in a set, but for a sequence this is a natural requirement.

3. Indexing. Again this is concerned with the order. It is common to assign to each element in a sequence a positive integer or *index*. The index of the first element in the sequence is 1, of the second is 2 and so on. Therefore the elements in the sequence can be referred to by identifying their index rather than by stating their contents.

   This indexing of elements in a sequence will be familiar to those who have written programs using arrays. An array of strings, integers or general records is simply a sequence of data items, stored one after the other, and indexed in a suitable way. In the example program shown below, we have a simple Pascal program which illustrates how a simple sequence of records of names and addresses may be stored in an array indexed by the integers from 1 to 10. (Figure 8.5)

8.16 Some sequence definitions using VDM

We may now formalise several of the above ideas using VDM statements. In order to do this, we shall need to use some standard definitions. These are:

len S = the number of elements in the sequence S

S(i) = the element of the sequence which has index i

We shall use these two definitions as the basis for our specifications.

8.16.1 Concatenation

Imagine that two hospitals have waiting lists for appointments to see a consultant, and one of the hospitals is closed. Then one possible scenario is that the two waiting lists are concatenated to form a single waiting list with all the patients from one hospital followed by all the patients from the other hospital.

If we think about the resulting list, what can we say about it?

Well, first of all, we can identify its length. The length of the new list is going to be the sum of the lengths of the two original lists. So if the original lists are called S_1 and S_2, then the new list, Newlist, say, satisfies len Newlist = len S_1 + len S_2.

But secondly, we may actually identify the indexes in Newlist of each of the items in S_1 and S_2. The items in S_1 will have the same index in Newlist, while the items in S_2 will have index in Newlist equal to the sum of their original index and the length of S_1. (If you cannot see that immediately, then try an example.)

We can use this thinking to specify the function Concat as follows:

Concat(S_1 :Patient*, S_2:Patient*) Newlist:Patient*

Post len Newlist = len S_1 + len S_2

$\wedge \forall i \leq len S_1, S_1(i)$ =Newlist(i)

$\wedge \forall j \leq$ len $S_2, S_2(j)$ =Newlist(len S_1 + j)

```
Pascal program to input 10 names and addresses and store
them in an array of records.

program StoreRecords;
const
    ListSize = 10;
type
   Person = Record
             name:string;
             Address : array[1..4] of string;
        end;
   List = array[1..ListSize] of Person;

Var
  OurList : List;
  i,j : integer;

begin
for i := 1 to ListSize do            {for each record in the list}
   begin
   writeln('Please enter name of person ',i);
   readln(OurList[i].name);
   writeln('Please enter address in four lines');
   for j := 1 to 4 do
      readln(OurList[i].Address[j]); {input name and
                                      address}
   end;
end.
```

Figure 8.5

8.16.2 Exercises

1. Suppose, in the previous example about hospital waiting lists, the decision was to have the names from Sequence S_2 preceding those from sequence S_1, what modifications would you need to make to the specification?

2. A fairer system might be to alternate names from the two sequences until the shorter sequence was exhausted. Try to write a specification for this possibility using VDM.

8.16.3 Finding the first and last items in a sequence

We now consider specifying two functions, one which yields the first item in a sequence, the other which yields the last. In this case, the difficulty will lie in defining the pre-conditions rather than the post-conditions, but the problem is in any case quite straightforward.

Firstitem(S:Item*) x:item
    Pre S $\neq$ []
    Post x = S(1)

Lastitem(S:Item*) x:item
    Pre S $\neq$ []
    Post i = ind(S) $\wedge$ x = S(i)

We can write similar specifications to give us the remaining items in the sequence after the head or tail has been deleted. These specifications display the same implicitness that we identified earlier in this chapter and also use the definitions of Firstitem and Lastitem.

Tail(S:item*) T:item*
    Pre S $\neq$ []
    Post S = Firstitem(S) $\rightarrow$ T

8.16.4 Exercise

Write a specification for a function Head, which acts on a sequence S and returns the sequence made up of all the items in S except the last item.

8.17   Proofs relating to sequences

It will come as no surprise to discover that one of the most important methods in proving results for sequences is the method of induction. In order to apply induction to a sequence, we shall again need a slightly new formulation of the method. Jones (1990) expresses sequence induction in the following way:

$$p([]) \; e \in X, \; t \in X^*, \; p(t) \vdash p(cons(e,t))$$
$$t \in X^* \vdash p(t)$$

In other words, to prove that a proposition $p(t)$ holds for an arbitrary sequence, t, of elements from a set X, we follow these steps:

1. Prove that the statement holds for the null sequence [].

2. Assume that the statement p holds for the arbitrary sequence t, and let e be an element of X.

3. Show that p holds for the sequence which consists of e followed by the sequence t.

4. Conclude that the statement p is true for arbitrary sequences t.

8.18   Application of induction for sequences

In this section, we shall think again about the implementation of the procedure for deleting an item from a list. Earlier in this chapter, we wrote the following specification for the process:

Remove(old:element)
    ext wr currentlist:list
pre old $\in$ currentlist
post currentlist =
    firstpart$^\frown$secondpart
    $\wedge currentlist$ = firstpart$^\frown$[old]$^\frown$secondpart

In figure 8.4, we claimed that the following program gave a realisation of this specification.

```
procedure Delete(X:string; L1:ListType; var L2:ListType);
var
    i:integer;
begin
    {A}
    i := 1; {start at first name in list}
    while (X ≠ L1[i]) {name not found}
    and (L1[i] ≠ '??????????') {end of list not reached}
    do begin
    L2[i] := L1[i]; {copy to new list}
    i := i + 1; {go on to next name in list}
    end;
    {B}
    while (L1[i] ≠ '??????????') do {end of list not reached}
    begin
    L2[i] := L1[i+1];
    i:= i+1;
    end;
    {C}
    L2[i] := '??????????'; {put end-of-list marker}
end;
```

(As before, we assume that a constant, ListSize, has been declared giving the maximum size of the list, and that the following type declaration has been made:

ListType = array[1..ListSize] of string;

The procedure has, as parameters, the name to be deleted (X) and the array containing the list (L1). The resulting new list is returned in a variable parameter (L2). A special string element, '??????????', is used to indicate when the end of the list is reached.)

Following the method described in the previous section, we shall now prove the correctness of the realisation.

We begin by stating the result which we wish to prove,

p(t) : the function Delete(x,t,t) is a valid realisation of Remove(x)

Note: Here the underlying list t is external to the process Remove and is implemented through the variable parameter L2 in the Pascal procedure Delete.

The proof proceeds as follows (we have chosen to give an informal description of the proof to show more clearly how the induction argument works in practice.):

1) We need to prove first that the statement holds for the null sequence []. Let the sequence be []. We may observe that old $\notin$ [] and so the definition of Remove does not apply since the pre-condition is not satisfied. Therefore there is nothing to prove for tbis case.

2) We assume that the statement p holds for the arbitrary sequence t, and we let e be an element of X. In other words, we are able to assume that the procedure Delete *is* a realisation of Remove for the sequence t. We must now show that p holds for the longer sequence which consists of e followed by the sequence t.

By the precondition for Remove, $x \in$ cons(e,t).

Therefore, either x=e or $x \in$ t.

If x = e then, by the program, the loop in {A} is never executed, and in loop {B} the content of t is copied to the result list. This is equivalent to the specification for Remove with firstpart nul and secondpart equal to t.

If $x \neq$ e (and therefore $x \in$ t), by the program the first pass of the loop at {A} will copy e to the first place in the result list. By the inductive hypothesis, execution of the remainder of the program appends the list t with entry x removed to the result list. This is most easily seen in the diagram (figure 8.6).

Note: The proof we have described here is not very convincing (although it is true) because the form of program written is not well-suited to the proof. The following program, written recursively, would be far better suited to a proof of satisfiability:

```
procedure RecDelete(X:string,L1:ListType, var L2:ListType);
var
    L3:ListType;
    i:integer;
```

```
begin
if L1[1]='??????????' then L2[1]='??????????'
else
    begin
    if L1[1]=X then for i:= 1 to ListSize-1 do L2[i]=L1[i+1]
    else
    begin
    for i:=1 to ListSize-1 do L3[i]=L1[i+1];
    RecDelete(X,L3,L3);
    L2[1]:=L1[1];
    for i:=1 to ListSize-1 do L2[i+1]=L3[i]
    end;
end;
```

8.19 Exercise

Write a specification for a function which checks whether a bank has an account holder whose name is stored as the variable *query*.

Note: Assume that the accounts are stored in sequence, ordered alphabetically by customer name.

Aim: To show that the procedure takes

L1 = | firstpart | |x| | secondpart |

and produces

L2 = | firstpart | | secondpart |

Suppose that we have L1 = |y| L*

    By our inductive hypothesis, if L* contains x then Delete(x,L*,L2) conforms to the specification.

Either: Or:

    x is the first entry in L1   x is not the first entry in L1

    L1 = |nul| |x| |tail| L1 = |y| |tail|

    L2 = |nul| |tail| |tail| = | firstpart | |x| | secondpart |

    i.e. is in the required form   (by the inductive hypothesis)

                                  L2 = |y| | firstpart | | secondpart |

                          i.e. is in the required form

Figure 8.6   The inductive proof of satisfiability.

Chapter 9

Data Reification and Operational Decomposition

9.1 Introduction

The principal feature of formal methods which we have identifed in this book is their ability to define formally the requirements of a system which can then be implemented in a way which can be proved rigorously to satisfy the specification. This obviates the need for testing and provides a program of provably high quality and reliability. Throughout the book we have given simple examples of the processes involved. This chapter is concerned particularly with the process of converting a specification in VDM for a *data structure* into an implementation. Data reification is the process whereby an **abstract** data specification is converted into a concrete implementation which is appropriate to the high level language in which we are working. **Operational decomposition** is concerned with producing the program code which is used for the *manipulation* of the data structure.

Wirth (1976) described the process of writing computer programs to be made up of defining and implementing algorithms combined with the appropriate data structures. In this chapter, we see data reification as the process of choosing the data structures. Operational decomposition corresponds to the process of implementing the algorithms.

9.2   The problem identified

Within the description of the specification for a system will be a description of the data which is to be stored. This data will be described in its *natural* way. Thus it may be described as a *set*, or a *sequence*, or *something else*.

Alongside this description of the data will come some description of the Pre- and Post- conditions relating to the various processing requirements for the data which is to be stored. Note that, under the rules which we have been following, neither the data specifications nor the descriptions of the processing should be concrete; thus neither should presume any particular *method* of implementation.

Our task, as a software engineer, is to choose appropriate methods for constructing the data structures and for realising the related functions and procedures in a selected high level language.

Therefore, we can view the situation as in figure 9.1. On the left hand side of the figure is the abstract definition. On the right hand side is the concrete implementation. Clearly, the intention is that the concrete implementation will reproduce accurately and faithfully all the aspects of the abstract definition.

This may be understood more easily if we compare the original specification of a new office with the design which is finally built. The original specification will probable describe the number of people who should be housed, and give some ideas about access and storage, but there will be many details of the design which will not appear on the original specification. (Figure 9.2)

As we have seen, the concrete and the abstract descriptions will not always be *equivalent* even though they represent the same fundamental solution to a problem. This is because the implementation will take account of redundancy in the specification, and may also introduce additional operations and structure to the data for convenience.

An example of this sort of thing arose in chapter 7, and we shall develop the discussion here. For example, a specification may identify the need for a sequence of data items to be stored. The implementation may choose to store these items using a linked list. So the specification and the fundamental design are indicated in figure 9.3. In practice, various processing of the data may be implemented more conveniently

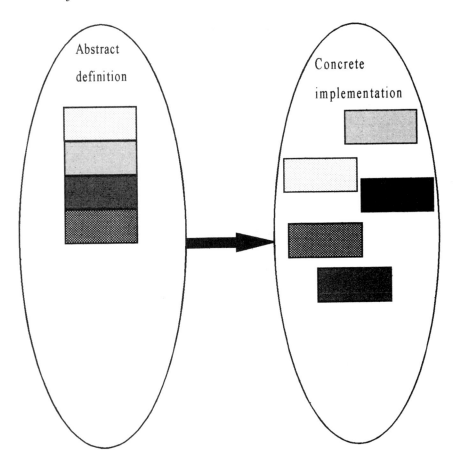

Figure 9.1 The concrete implementation contains all the requirements of the abstract definition, but may also include extra features

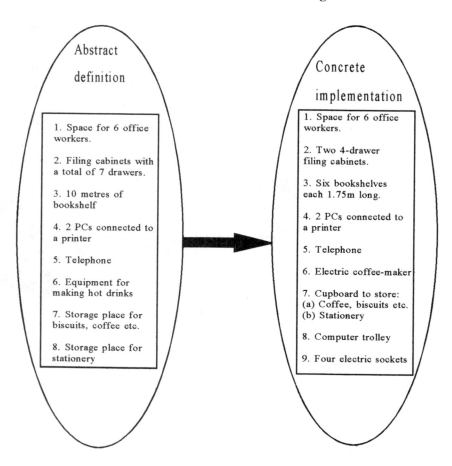

Figure 9.2 The original specification of a new office suite contains a list of requirements. The concrete implementation includes all these, but also includes other features which are determined by other factors.

if there are links backwards as well as forwards, and therefore the final implementation may be in the form of figure 9.4.

We have used the term *satisifiability* previously in this book. Satisfiability is the term used to describe those implementations which are correct, or, to be more accurate, satisfy their specifications. In order that an implementation of a data structure satisfies its specification, we shall insist on the following two properties:

1. The existence of a *retrieve function*: this is used to retrieve the original value as it maps to the original (abstract) specification from the implemented version.

For example, figure 9.5 illustrates a correspondence between the days of the week and the whole numbers between 1 and 7. A retrieve function would give the appropriate day of the week from the corresponding number.

2. The *adequacy* of the implementation: the implementation is adequate if it admits at least one concrete representation of each abstract value.

Looking again at figure 9.5 we can see that the implementation is adequate since there is one numerical value which corresponds to each day of the week.

9.3 Public Library Example

It is useful at this point to consider the extent to which our final implementation of the solution to a problem matches the problem *as it is initially described by the client*.

In implementing a public library system, it is clear that the books and borrowers details must be held and processed in various ways. Now this information may be conveyed to the systems analysts making the initial investigations in a variety of forms, but one which might arise is:

'A list of borrowers is to be maintained'

This is precisely the form of the statement which we gave in chapter 4.

This statement uses the term *list* to refer to what should, in fact, be described as a set. There is no reason why the librarian should be concerned with the order in which the system actually stores the details

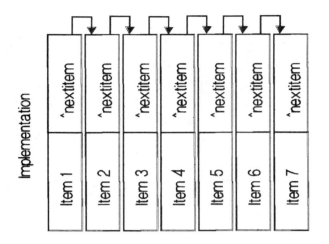

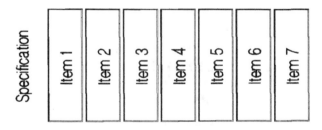

Figure 9.3 A linked list could be used to implement storage of a sequence of data items

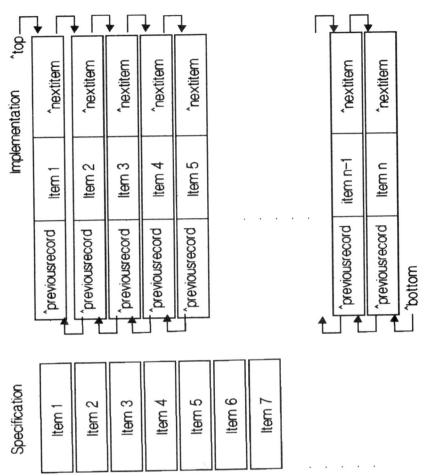

Figure 9.4 A sequence of data items may be more conveniently implemented using a doubly linked-list

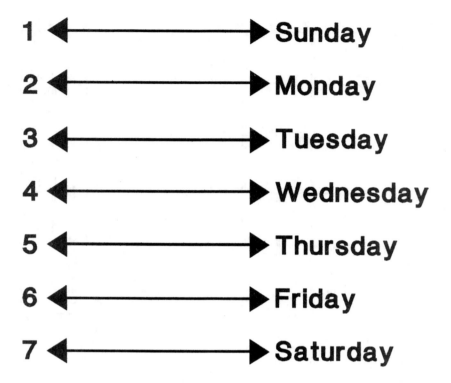

Figure 9.5 A correspondence may be established between the integers 1,2,3,...,7 and the days of the week.

of the borrowers, although there may well be preferences which need to be expressed about the order in which particular processing should be performed.

So during the first stage of the analysis, the systems analyst will attempt to make details of the specification clear. This will involve moving from the concrete description of the way things *might* be stored to a formal abstract definition of exactly what *must* be stored. The details of the processing requirements are held in a similarly abstract way.

The work of data reification is then concerned with taking the abstract descriptions and combining them in a suitable way. This must allow for the processing required and provide an adequate implementation with a suitable retrieve function.

Figure 9.6 illustrates how the user may be encouraged to view the system as a black box. The user is then unconcerned about how the internal parts of the system work. On the other hand, the user does need to be concerned to ensure that the contents of the black box are appropriate and function correctly.

9.4 Exercises

1. A programmer decides to represent the months of the year by the numbers 1,2,...,12. Draw a diagram which illustrates a retrieve function from this implementation to the abstract data set. Is the representation adequate?

2. A programmer records the number of books borrowed by a member of a public library as an integer between 1 and 5. Why is this representation a poor choice?

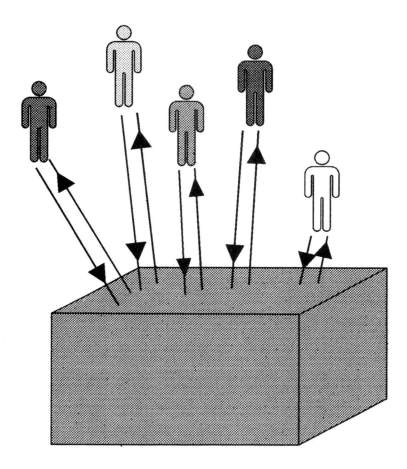

**Figure 9.6 The users see the system from the point of view
of the input required and the output produced, rather than
the detail of its internal operation.**

Chapter 10

Software Prototyping

10.1 Introduction

This chapter is concerned with the prototyping of software solutions to problems. We begin the discussion by considering why software prototyping is an attractive proposition, and we identify some general issues which arise when considering prototyping. We then describe various approaches to software prototyping, focusing particularly on those which apply formal methods.

10.2 What is prototype software?

In mechanical engineering, the term prototype is used to refer to a pre-production model of a proposed new product. When the product actually goes into production, many will be built and so a few prototype models are made so that the performance and features of the prototypes can be tested and any changes in design can be made before mass production is commenced. Thus prototype cars, for example, will cost considerably more to build than a production vehicle, but the savings made by making changes to the design before production commences are enormous. (See figures 10.1 & 10.2).

Software is not normally mass-produced. While the aim is still to use a prototype to help inform the design process, it is essential that the prototype software should be cheaply and quickly produced. Therefore

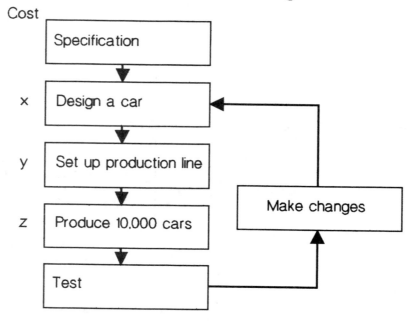

Cost

Total cost $=n(x+y+z)$, where n is the number of times changes are required

Figure 10.1 Production of 10,000 cars without prototyping

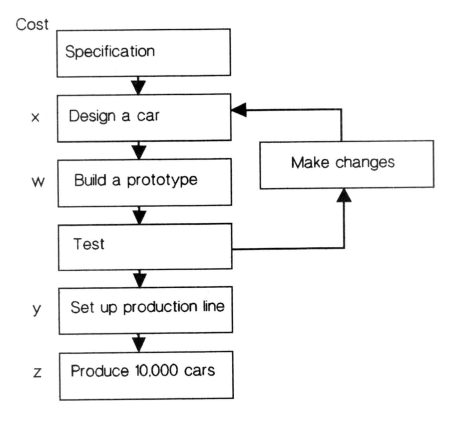

Total cost $= n(x+w)+y+z$, where n is
the number of times changes are
required

Figure 10.2 Production of 10,000 cars with prototyping

prototyping in software engineering is slightly different from conventional engineering prototyping since the performance of the prototype may not be as good as performance of the final version, and this may be a deliberate choice. (Figures 10.3 & 10.4)

The following list of features of prototype software is adapted from a list given by Hekmatpour and Ince (1988):

- It is a system which works, and not just a drawing or design

- It may be a throw-away model of the actual system, or it may be a first step in an evolutionary approach to systems development

- It must be built quickly and cheaply

- It is part of a development process which includes evaluation and modification.

10.3   Why prototype software?

From the beginning, this book has been concerned with methods of improving the quality of software which is developed. We identified software engineering methods in general as being appropriate as a way of improving software quality and we then focused upon the accurate and exhaustive **specification** of requirements as being the key to successful completion of a software development project.

Software specifications need to be clearly and unambiguously presented, and this has motivated much of our discussion of formal methods. However, there is another factor which can be still more significant than clarity and unambiguity in the specification, and that is the issue of validity. In other words, are the definitions and specifications of the software which is to be developed appropriate for the task in hand: that is, are we building the right product?

Making sure that the specification demonstrates faithfully the requirements of the client is the fundamental role of systems analysts in the investigation process, but inevitably their clients often find it hard to describe in words just what their needs are. No less difficult is the problem of looking at the written specifications drawn up by the

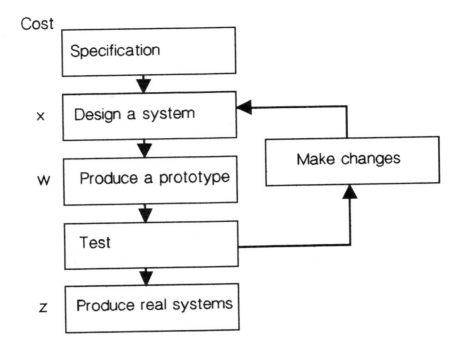

Total cost =n(x+w)+z, where n is the
number of times changes are required.
Typically, in software production, z would
be extremely small compared with x and w.
So, if a fully-working prototype is produced,
the cost will be very high.

**Figure 10.3 Software production using fully-functional
prototypes**

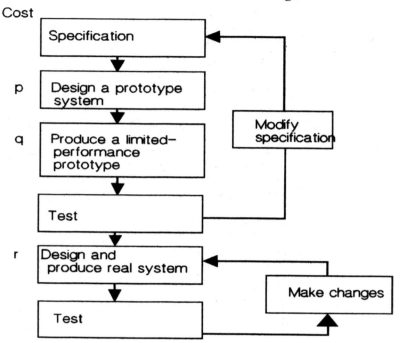

Total cost $= m(p+q)+nr$, where m is the
number of changes required to the
specification, and n is the number of
changes required to implement the final
specification. Typically, in software
production, p would be fairly small
compared with r. So, a limited-
performance prototype is very useful
in avoiding the necessity for re-designing
a working system should the original
specification prove unsatisfactory.

**Figure 10.4 Software may be produced more cheaply using
limited performance prototypes**

analysts or software engineers and seeing whether or not the technical description matches the users' needs. The clients or users understand what the programs should look like and how they should perform, but diagrams and text describing the specification can be almost meaningless.

Therefore it can be helpful to provide the users or clients with an early prototype system which exhibits many of the features of the specified system in order that the system can be tried out and problems with the specification can be identified at this early stage. The problem is, *How do we produce a prototype system at high speed and minimum cost?*

10.4   Other uses of prototype software

Apart from improving the requirements analysis, and hence the software specification, there can be a number of other reasons for providing a prototype solution to a problem. Hekmatpour and Ince (1988) provide a list which includes:

- Studying the feasibility and appropriateness of a systems design
- Comparing and contrasting the merits of rival designs.
- Demonstrating that a design meets the specification
- Resolving uncertainty as to whether computerisation will fit a particular application.
- Testing human-computer interfaces
- Implementing one-shot applications (i.e. programs which are only run once and then discarded)
- As a step in evolutionary software development.

10.5   Elementary software prototyping

Exactly how difficult it is to develop prototypes is dependent upon the nature of the project. For projects which are 'standard', it may be possible to produce a prototype with relative ease, whereas for a more individual project, prototyping may be more difficult.

10.5.1   Applications package based programming

Some standard software can assist the prototyping process. Therefore, when software is developed using a standard package, such as a database package it may be possible for a naive system to be established very rapidly and then refined to the user's particular needs. It is this later refinement which takes the time in development terms, and which makes the program really satisfactory in use. (Refer to our earlier discussion of quality in computer software, and the role of the non-functional requirements) Nevertheless, the early and unrefined version gives the client an idea of the 'feel' of the software. (Figure 10.5).

10.5.2   Programming based on high level language: use of libraries

High level language programmers are becoming increasingly aware of the need to store and re-use parts of programs which are widely applicable. Therefore new programs may be developed by using procedures which were originally written to perform the same tasks in other applications. The procedures are added to a library of routines available for re-use. As with the use of software applications packages to speed up the development process, re-use of code can be a very great asset in producing a rapid example system, even if the library procedures do not perform exactly according to the specification. As in the previous case, the important thing about a prototype is that it helps the client to think through exactly what it is that should have been specified in the first place. (Figure 10.6).

A similar approach uses bought-in standard library routines which are commercially available for developing programs. These share many of the advantages of re-using program code, while also giving a wider variety of facilities than any individual programmer would be likely to have developed and a guarantee of quality and reliability from the

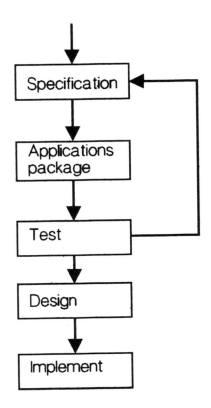

Figure 10.5 Using an applications package may enable a limited-performance prototype to be produced quickly and cheaply

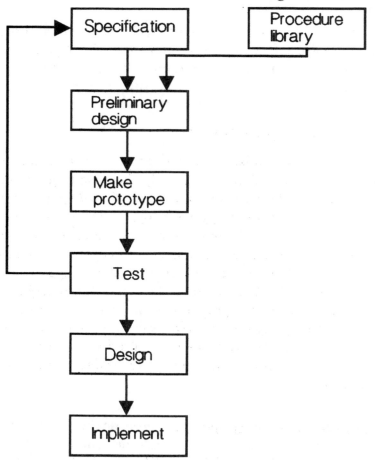

**Figure 10.6 Using a library of procedures may enable a
prototype to be produced quickly and cheaply**

supplier. These techniques are particularly encouraged when programs are to be developed using a high level language which promotes the use of library facilities (such as C or Modula-2) (see Ford (1990b) for further details).

10.5.3 Program generators

There are a number of specialised 'program generators' available which will write programs automatically. Typically they use a questionnaire approach to determine the answers to a series of questions about the application and then to write the actual code. In theory at least, the programs developed in this way could be used *live* and so the idea behind these program generators is attractive, but they tend to be rather less satisfactory in practice than the advertising might suggest. In particular, their area of applications tends to be rather limited, since they can usually generate efficiently programs of a particular type. Their efficiency in generating programs which are actually usable is questionable, but they are nevertheless valuable in the production of prototypes and the prototype programs can sometimes be re-coded to give the final versions. (Figure 10.7).

10.5.4 Screen generators

A method which uses screen generation software can be attractive. Screen generation software allows for the design of input and output screen to be completed without any of the processing of data being implemented. Clearly it is somewhat quicker and easier than other prototyping methods since it ignores altogether the question of processing which has to happen in a particular program, and concentrates instead upon the user interface. Users typically have a good understanding of the data requirements of a system and the values which they would expect to have to input, and of the forms of output which they would be likely to need. Therefore the use of screen generators is a very much simplified approach to prototyping since we produce the forms of input and output and give the users the opportunity to comment upon the result. This is the cheapest, but also the least reliable form of prototyping.

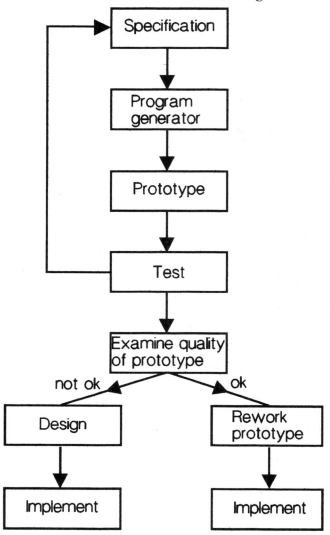

**Figure 10.7 A program generator may be used to produce a
prototype system**

10.6 Software specification and prototyping

The ideas of prototyping which we have met here are all based upon the belief that the use of a prototype system will assist in clearing up any doubts about the validity of the specification of the software which is to be developed. It is therefore important that the prototype system reproduces faithfully the specification which is currently available, since any mismatch between the prototype and the specification might go unnoticed and leave a serious deficiency in the final system.

10.6.1 Software specification, CASE tools and prototyping

One of the aids to documenting a software engineering project which we have not discussed in the present work is the use of a CASE tool. CASE tools come in various forms, and a fuller discussion of their facilities may be found elsewhere (for example Sommerville (1989), Gane (1990)). Software specifications may be prepared by the use of a CASE tool and they are then checked by the CASE tool's facilities. This checking ensures, among other things, consistency in the use and definitions of the various entities within the project. Some CASE tools have additional facilities for the production of the actual code needed for the programs in suitable languages. Therefore an option might be available to select code generation and produce a prototype system almost directly from entering the details of the specification into the CASE tool. (Figure 10.8).

10.7 Evolutionary prototyping

We have mentioned ideas which relate to evolutionary prototyping several times in this chapter already. This technique contrasts with the more normal 'throw it away' prototyping with which we are normally concerned. Most of our prototypes have been assumed to have been designed in order to test something specific and to ensure that the

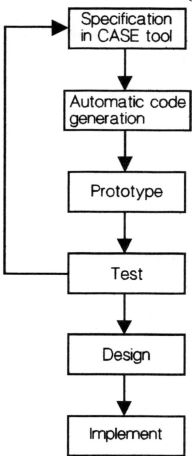

**Figure 10.8 Using an CASE tool may enable a prototype to be
produced quickly and cheaply**

specification or the design is appropriate before the final version of the software is produced at considerable expense.

Evolutionary prototyping adopts a completely different strategy, by assuming that software requirements are *dynamic* and will change frequently. Therefore, it is argued, the idea of finally producing a complete and accurate specification for the solution at some point in time, and then expecting the solution proposed to be satisfactory in the longer term is rather unrealistic. Instead, the software development process becomes *iterative* to reflect the dynamic nature of the requirements. The system is constantly re-evaluated, re-designed and re-implemented and each iteration provides a prototype for developing the next. (Figure 10.9).

It may be that eventually a final version could be arrived at, in which case the final iteration may form the basis of the finished software, but equally important is the fact that the stages in the process can be used, and therefore this evolutionary approach depends for its success on ensuring that each version of the system is actually functional and can be used as the current system. This is rather different from the tolerance of poorly implemented systems in the throw it away approach.

Also sometimes known as evolutionary prototyping is a system more correctly known as incremental prototyping, where a system is prototyped a section at a time. (See Hekmatpour and Ince (1988).)

10.8   Formal methods and prototyping

This book is really concerned with Formal Methods, and so far in this chapter we have discussed prototyping without mentioning formal methods. However, we have identified the software specification as the key in the development of prototypes, and we know that formal methods provide a good means to express specifications. We return now to consider how software development based upon VDM applies to our present discussion of prototyping.

In developing software using VDM, we identified in chapter 4 the following steps:

- specify the system formally

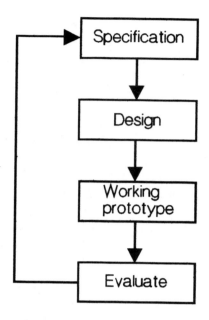

Figure 10.9 Evolutionary Prototyping

- prove that the specification is consistent

- do

  1. refine and decompose the specification
  2. prove that the realisation satisfies the previous specification

- until the realisation is as concrete as a program

- revise the above steps.

These are the steps involved in moving from *any* specification written in VDM to a realisation based upon a programming language, and just how long it will take to develop the program will depend upon the number of iterations of the steps labelled 1 & 2 involved in the process. Clearly, the more like VDM is the programming language of implementation, the fewer steps there will be in the process of conversion. On the other hand, from our earlier description of VDM, we can see that since VDM is designed to help us to make specifications which are independent of any particular implementation environment, it is unlikely that we will be able to find any appropriate language for implementation which is especially close to VDM.

For prototyping, the *speed* of development of the software prototype is much more important than the quality and *performance* of the final product. Therefore, it could be that some compromises are possible in the production of prototype software, even though these compromises would be inappropriate in the production of the final product. Hekmatpour and Ince (1988) describe the language EPROL which is a special prototyping language which has been designed to be as close as possible to VDM. The use of EPROL permits a very short time for development from specification to prototype, since the EPROL language is based around VDM.

The major changes necessary in the prototyping process are to move away from some of the implicitness of some of the function specifications in VDM towards a more explicit realisation of the functions themselves. Thus, the use of EPROL for the prototype production provides precisely the prototyping speed which we seek.

Why, if EPROL is such a good way of implementing prototype solutions to problems, should we persist in writing the final version of the software using either a conventional high level language, or an applications package?

For the answer to this fundamental question, we would need to turn to the question of the different qualities of programming and software development environments. There are many books on this subject (for example Ford (1990b), Gane (1990)) . For the present, it is sufficient to identify the distinction between the use of EPROL to represent some sort of implementation which is faithful to the specification, and the desire to produce a final working system which is as efficient as possible.

This is highlighted in the original software specification where there are a list of non-functional requirements. In chapter 2 we saw that non-functional requirements were precisely those aspects of a software package which formed the basis of a user's judgement on the *quality* of the package. Questions such as how quickly the software runs, and how easy it is to use are important to the user. These sorts of issues are not so important to the prototyper (although design of the user interface can and should be important within the prototype). Therefore in producing the final version of the program, it is important to consider *all* the possible software development strategies available to the software engineer as well as attractive easy options such as marketing the existing prototype solution.

10.9   The cost of prototyping

One of the arguments which can be levelled against the use of software prototyping is that it is expensive. This argument may not be true, but it is very difficult to provide a convincing reason to explain why it is not!

The argument against prototyping is based upon the following:

1. Under the throw-it-away prototype system the development of a prototype is an additional stage in the software development process which is otherwise unnecessary. Therefore the conclusion drawn is that it is wasteful.

2. Prototyping may not really be very much faster than developing the system itself, and if the prototyping medium is very different, as in the case of prototyping languages such as EPROL, then the work involved in producing the prototype will save no time in developing the final system.

3. Prototyping delays the start of implementation of the final system. In an industry where delays in the delivery of completed software projects is a major problem, introducing a clear cause of additional delay is unattractive.

Arguments which may be made in favour of prototyping are as follows:

1. Prototyping improves the completeness and accuracy of the specification of the program. Therefore the final result may be of higher quality than would otherwise be the case.

2. If the specification is more accurate, then the amount of time spent on maintenance may be reduced. This should be set against the generally accepted statistic that between 50 and 90 per cent of software costs arise out of maintenance of the software. If we are able to reduce this time wasted, then there will be clear cost savings.

3. Staff can be trained and can provide early evaluation of a new system using the prototype. It can be that the actual live running of the system can actually commence at an earlier date because staff training can be completed before the program is really ready.

4. Prototype systems which are completely functional can be used. Therefore it might be possible to offer a client the availability of a low specification working system at an early date, with the completed and fully functional system following later when it is complete.

5. Prototype systems do not necessarily need to be thrown away and therefore time spent on their development is not necessarily wasted. Evolutionary prototyping is one example where prototyping forms an integral part of the development of a system.

As can be seen from these arguments for and against prototyping, the problem of persuading clients of the wisdom of prototyping is that the potential gains from its use, while possibly great, are intangible. On the other hand, the costs of prototyping are immediately clear. Furthermore, the occasions when prototypes yield the greatest gains in the software development process, are the occasions when the initial design has a major flaw. But these are the occasions when the initial prototype is rejected by the client and a second prototype needs to be produced. Therefore the greatest gains from prototyping happen when the use of the prototype seems to cause even greater cost!

The use of CASE tools which provide prototype systems almost automatically, and therefore at minimal cost, or of languages such as EPROL which are based closely upon the work already completed in the formal specification of the system is therefore clearly attractive, since it keeps costs of prototyping to a minimum. This is seen by some people in the software development industry as one of the principal benefits to be derived, on the one hand, from the use of a CASE tool, or, on the other hand, from the use of a formal method such as VDM.

Chapter 11

Using Formal Methods

11.1 Introduction

This final chapter focuses on the three important questions:

- What are formal methods used for?

- Who should use formal methods?

- How can I learn more about formal methods?

11.2 What are formal methods used for?

Much of our discussion so far has been based upon theoretical rather than practical applications of formal methods techniques. We have chosen our examples to be as realistic and to come from such familiar data processing applications areas as has been possible, but we have nevertheless avoided working through any complete example programs using formal methods.

There are two reasons for this. One reason is that this book is intended to introduce the ideas of formal methods to as wide a readership as possible. It has not been our intention to prepare the reader to use formal methods in practical situations, but rather to gain some insight into what they are and how they might be helpful. Furthermore, it is important to emphasise repeatedly the way in which the use of formal methods is implementation independent, and therefore too great a focus upon writing actual programs would be unhelpful.

The second reason is that formal methods have been more widely applied in theoretical and laboratory-based research work than they have in real data processing applications. The resons for this lack of popularity are manifold. We list a few of those most often given:

1. Many programmers do not know about formal methods.

2. Some people who have tried to use formal methods find them hard to understand because of their mathematical background.

3. The use of formal methods usually slows down initial progress in software development. Even though the quality of the software produced and the speed of later stages in the process may be increased, there is nevertheless reluctance to adopt a seemingly expensive approach.

4. Many software developers are satisfied with existing methods of software development and see no reason to change their practices.

Nevertheless, there are good examples of real systems which have been developed using Formal Methods, and we refer the reader to descriptions of these. (See, for example, Hekmatpour & Ince (1988), Jones & Shaw (1990) and Sommerville (1989)). We turn now to consider the question of how to determine whether or not formal methods are an appropriate tool for software development in particular projects.

11.3   Who should use Formal Methods?

It would be simple and attractive for us to simply state that formal methods are such an indespensible tool in quality software development that every software development should adopt them for every project. However, we are realistic enough to accept that this is very far from reality today. In practice, for the reasons which were given in the preceding section, there will be many arguments against the use of formal methods in particular projects. In this section we shall attempt to weigh the advantages against the disadvantages for various types of project and to deduce some broad rules to apply.

The principal arguments which we will accept against the use of formal methods are arguments based upon

- cost

- the time taken to develop software

- the availability of suitably qualified and experienced staff.

There is little that can be done about the last of these three, at least in the short term. If a software developer is faced with a project and no staff available who are competent in formal techniques, then there is no alternative but to develop the software by more conventional means. The only observation which we can make is that perhaps in the future somebody will write a book which makes the concept of formal methods more attractive!

We move on to consider the questions of cost and software development time. The advantages of using formal methods which we have identified throughout this book have hinged around the ideas that they provide a clearer way to express unambiguously the requirements of a new system and that therefore thay improve the quality of the software developed, since it is more likely to meet the specification intended. We also identified the reduced testing and maintenance times as being further advantages. We are therefore faced with the problem of weighing the advantages of any improvement in software quality, alongside any financial saving in testing and maintenance against the probable cost in producing software (arguably) more slowly and at higher initial development cost. (Figure 11.1).

The biggest hurdle to overcome in this comparison stems from the fact that much of the cost involved is intangible and therefore impossible to calculate exactly:

- How many rewrites of the program might we have needed if the initial specification had been incorrect?

- How do we measure the *higher quality* of the finished software, and how do we place a monetary value on it?

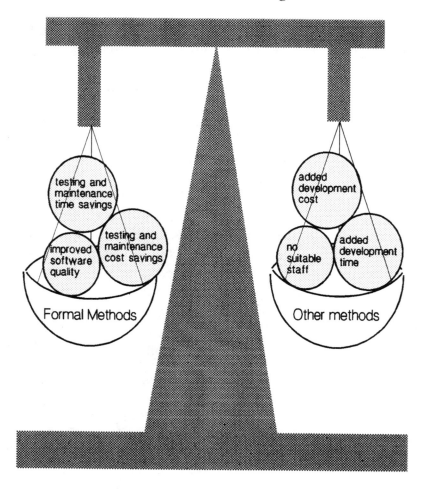

Figure 11.1 Factors which need to be balanced when deciding whether or not to use formal methods.

- To what extent are improvements in software quality the result of formal techniques and to what extent are other factors coming into the equation

The result of all this is that it becomes very difficult to give any clear and confident statement about the savings and benefits likely to accrue from the use of formal methods.

However, despite all this we can come to some fairly confident conclusions about some occasions when it would be *inappropriate* to attempt to apply formal methods:

1. When a program is very simple. Program with very simple specifications can be clearly understood by everybody. Therefore there is little point in spending a lot of time in writing a formal specification which simply expresses, in a formal way, facts which could more easily and directly be described informally.

2. When a program is to be based upon an existing program with very minor modifications. Sometimes, we have an exisiting program which is required in a slightly modified form. If the original program had a formal definition and specification which could be adapted to the new case, then it would be worthwhile to do this. However, if the original program is largely satisfactory and the scale of the changes which are to be made are relatively small, the benefits of formal specification are unlikely to equal the costs.

3. Programs where the speed of completion is more important than accuracy. This could for example apply in a one-off program which is needed in a hurry to try to answer a particular problem. If the program is needed immediately or will be of no use, then formal methods are unlikely to provide a sensible approach.

There are also some circumstances where the importance of software quality and reliability is paramount. In these situations it becomes sensible to employ whatever quality development methods are available, including whenever appropriate, the use of formal methods.

1. Defence projects are very important, since they deal with the life of the people who use them. Guided missile control systems,

aircraft autopilot systems and similar projects are undertaken at high cost and can justify the expense of highly sophisticated and reliable software development.

2. Other safety-critical projects come into a similar category. So, for example, the programs which control a nuclear power plant or a hospital intensive care unit would naturally be prepared with great attention to software quality and reliability. The use of formal methods and other quality assurance techniques is clearly justified in these applications.

But between these two extremes there are many software projects where it is inconvenient, but not life-threatening, if software quality is low. There may even be clear financial loss if errors are made. Here the choice between the use of a formal method and other approaches is much less clear. It will be influenced as much by management prejudices, the size of the development budget, and the aspirations of the software team, as by more appropriate factors such as the likely cost of future maintenance, the life of the software and the potential for re-use of the procedures within the programs.

11.4   Exercise

For each of the following applications, decide how important the use of high quality software development methods will be:

1. The development of a program to test a young person's spellings.

2. The development of a program to control borrowing of books from a public library

3. The development of a program which keeps customer account details for a bank

4. The development of a stock-control program for a mail order catalogue company

5. The development of a program which gives dietary advice to sick people.

11.5 How can I learn more formal methods?

We hope that as a result of reading this book, you will want to know more about formal methods, and that you will want to develop your skills in this area so that they can be applied in future software development projects. Jones (1990) is the book which we would recommend for further reading on VDM, and the book Jones & Shaw (1990) gives examples of applications. Hekmatpour & Ince (1988) shows the relationship with prototyping in much more detail than we have considered it here and also demonstrates how VDM can be used in a realistic case study based around the development of prototypes.

If you are unfamiliar with the ideas which underpin software engineering, then we recommend Sommerville (1989) as a good thorough introduction, which also discusses the language Z which is an alternative formal specification language to VDM. For the reader interested in pursuing Z, a number of other books concerned with the Z language are becoming available.

The bibliographies of all the books listed give further references to research papers which may also be of interest.

Appendix I
Solutions to selected exercises &
Example computer programs

Chapter 2
2.4.1
The following lists give examples of the functional and non-functional requirements of a system to operate a bank's accounts. They are by no means exhaustive.

Functional requirements:
1. A list shall be kept of all account holders.
2. Details shall be kept of all accounts held by each customer including:
- The type of account
- The current state of the account
- Recent transactions involving the account
3. The bank's employees shall be able to obtain information concerning individual accounts from the system.
4. A bank statement shall be sent to each account holder at regular intervals or on request.
5. Non-functional requirements:
6. The system shall be easy to use
7. A bank statement shall be issued within one day of a request
8. The current balance in an account shall be available within 30 seconds

Chapter 4

4.3.4.1

1. $y = x \times x$ (Specification)

2. Infer $y = x^2$

4.3.4.2

1. $x \in R$, $x \neq 0$ (Pre-condition)
2. $x > 0$ or $x < 0$
3. from $x > 0$

       (a)$y = +1$ (specification)

       (b) deduce $(x > 0) \wedge (y = +1)$

4.from $x \langle 0$

       (a) $y = -1$

       (b) infer $(x \langle 0) \wedge (y = -1)$

5.infer

$\{(x > 0) \wedge (y = +1)\} \vee \{(x < 0) \wedge (y = -1)\}$

4.3.4.3

The pre-condition is necessary in order to ensure that x has a real square root.

1.$x \geq 0$ (pre-condition)

2. Deduce $+\sqrt{x} \in \Re$

3.$+\sqrt{x} \rangle 0$ (definition of$+\sqrt{x}$)

4.$(+\sqrt{x})^2 = x$ (definition of $\sqrt{x}$)

5. Deduce $(y^2 = x) \wedge (y \geq 0)$

4.3.4.4

1. From $x \in y$

      search = *true*

2. Deduce $(x \in y) \wedge (search = true)$

3. From $x \notin y$

      search = *false*

4. Deduce $(x \notin y) \wedge (search = false)$

5. From 2 and 4 deduce

      $\{(x \in y) \wedge (search = true)\} \vee \{x \notin y) \wedge (search = false)\}$

Chapter 5

5.10.1

Implicit specification of function $y \in \Re$

PRE: True

POST: $y^2 + 3y + 2 = 0$

5.10.2

first(list: list of names): name

PRE: list is not empty

POST: $\forall x \in list: (first$ comes before x alphabetically$) \vee (x = first)$

5.10.4

first(list: list of names):name
PRE: list is not empty
POST:

>first = name at top of list
>if there are more names on the list:
>>compare first with next name on list
>>if next name belongs before first replace first with next name
>>go on to next name
>
>continue until no more names

Chapter 6

6.3

program Sorter;
type
    ListType = array[1..10] of string; {A longer list is theoretically
                                         possible, but requires a large
                                         amount of memory in your machine}
var
    ListSize:integer;
    NameList:ListType;

```pascal
procedure InputNames;
var currentname : string;
begin
writeln('Type in list of names. Type "**" to stop');
ListSize := 0;
repeat
    ListSize := ListSize+1;
    readln(currentname);
    NameList[ListSize] := CurrentName;
until CurrentName= '**';
ListSize := ListSize-1;
end;

procedure OutPutnames;
var
  i:integer;
begin
for i := 1 to ListSize do
writeln(i,':  ',NameList[i]);
readln;
end;

procedure SortN(n:integer;var list:ListType);
var
  TempList:ListType;
  FirstIndex,i:integer;
  First:string;
```

```
function FirstName:integer;
var
  First,NextName:string;
  i,j:integer;
begin
i := 2;
j := 1;
First := list[1];
Nextname := list[2];
repeat
    if NextName < First then
      begin
      First := NextName;
      j := i;
      end;
    i := i+1;
    NextName := list[i];
until i>n;
FirstName:=j;
end;


begin   {SortN}
if n > 1 then
  begin
  FirstIndex := FirstName;
  First := List[FirstIndex];
  for i := 1 to FirstIndex-1 do
    TempList[i] := List[i];
```

```
      for i := FirstIndex+1 to n do
         TempList[i-1] := List[i];
      for i := 1 to n-1 do
      SortN(n-1,TempList);
      List[1] := First;
      for i := 2 to n do
         List[i] := TempList[i-1];
      end;
   end;  {SortN}


begin
InputNames;
SortN(ListSize,NameList);
OutPutNames;
end.
```

6.9.1
For n=1,

$$1^2 + 2^2 + \ldots + n^2 = 1$$

$$n(n+1)(2n+1)/6 = 1 \times 2 \times 3/6$$
$$= 1$$

So formula is true for n=1
Suppose that it is true for n=1,2,...,N. Then

$$1^2 + 2^2 + ... + N^2 = N(N+1)(2N+1)/6$$

$$So, \ 1^2 + 2^2 + ... + (N+1)^2 = N(N+1)(2N+1)/6 + (N+1)^2$$

$$= \{N(N+1)(2N+1) + 6(N+1)(N+1)\}/6$$

$$= (N+1)\{(2N^2+N) + (6N+6)\}/6$$

$$= (N+1)(2N^2+7N+6)/6$$

$$Also, \ (N+1)(N+1+1)(2(N+1)+1)/6 = (N+1)(N+2)(2N+3)/6$$

$$= (N+1)\{2N^2+7N+6\}/6$$

Therefore, $1^2 + 2^2 + ... + N^2 + (N+1)^2 = (N+1)(N+1+1)(2(N+1)+1)/6$
So, if the formula is true for n=N it is also true for n=N+1. It is true for
n=1. Therefore it is true for all $n \geq 1$.

6.9.2
For n=1,

$$1^3 + 2^3 + ... + n^3 = 1$$

$$n^2(n+1)^2/4 = 4/4$$

$$= 1$$

So formula is true for n=1.

Suppose formula is true for n=N. Then,

$$1^3 + 2^3 + \ldots + N^3 = N^2(N+1)^2/4$$
$$so, \; 1^3 + 2^3 + \ldots + N^3 + (N+1)^3 = N^2(N+1)^2/4 + (N+1)^3$$
$$= (N+1)^2\{N^2 + 4(N+1)\}/4$$
$$= (N+1)^2(N+2)^2/4$$
$$= (N+1)^2(N+1+1)^2/4$$

So, if formula is true for n=N it is also true for n=N+1. Formula is true for n=1. Therefore it is true for all $n \geq 1$.

6.11

Pascal program using recursion to find the highest paid employee from a list. This program is written in Turbo Pascal version 5.5.

```
program FindHighestPaid;
type
    EmployeePointer = ^Employee;
    Employee =    record
                name: string;
                salary:integer;
                Next:EmployeePointer
                end;
var
    First,Highest:EmployeePointer;
```

```
Function HigherPaid(x,y:EmployeePointer):EmployeePointer;
begin
if x^.salary >=y^.salary then HigherPaid := x
else HigherPaid := y;
end;


Function HighestPaid(HeadOfList:EmployeePointer): EmployeePointer;
var
    ThisEmployee,NextEmployee:EmployeePointer;
begin
ThisEmployee := HeadOfList;
NextEmployee := ThisEmployee^.next;
if NextEmployee = nil then HighestPaid := ThisEmployee
else HighestPaid :=
HigherPaid(ThisEmployee,HighestPaid(NextEmployee));
end;


procedure InputEmployees(var first:EmployeePointer);
var
    ThisEmployee,NextEmployee:EmployeePointer;
    stop : boolean;
    Answer : string;
begin
ThisEmployee :=nil;
stop := false;
```

```
repeat
    new(NextEmployee);
    writeln('enter employee''s name');
    readln(NextEmployee^.name);
    writeln('enter salary');
    readln(NextEmployee^.salary);
    NextEmployee^.next := nil;
    If ThisEmployee = nil then first := NextEmployee
    else ThisEmployee^.next :=NextEmployee;
    ThisEmployee := NextEmployee;
    writeln('Do you wish to enter another employee record?');
    readln(answer);
    if answer <> 'yes' then stop := true;
until stop;
end;

begin
InputEmployees(First);
Highest := HighestPaid(First);
writeln('Highest paid employee is ',highest^.name,' with a salary of
',highest^.salary);
writeln('Press RETURN to continue');
readln;
end.
```

6.13.1
(a,1) for any value of a
(2,2), (3,4), (4,6), (5,8), ... etc.

6.13.2

a. True.

Proof:

1. $a \in Z^+$
2. addup(1) = 1   Post-addup(a)
3. addup(a) = 1+2+3+...+a   Inductive hypothesis
4. addup(a+1)=a+1+addup(a)   definition of addup
5. addup(a+1)=a+1+1+2+...+a   subs 3
6. addup(a+1)=1+2+3+...+a+1
7. infer addup(a) by N-induction

b. False: no specification is given for Factorial(1)

c. False: e.g. Add2(2)=$2 \times 4 \div 2 = 4$

Chapter 7

7.11.1

ADDSQUARE

Ext wr n, wr SQ_n

Post $SQ_n = 1^2 + 2^2 + 3^2 + ... + n^2$

7.11.2

Ext rd AccountDataBase : set of account records, wr FredSmithRecs: set of account records

post

$\{FredSmith \operatorname{Re} cs \subseteq AccountDataBase\}$

$\wedge \{[(x \in FredSmith \operatorname{Re} cs) \wedge (x.name = 'Fred\ Smith')]$

$\vee [(x \notin FredSmith \operatorname{Re} cs) \wedge (x.name \neq 'Fred\ Smith')]\}$

Chapter 8
8.14.1

queue = element*

AddToQueue(new:element)
ext wr : currentlist:queue
post currentlist = *currentlist* ⃗[new]

RemoveFromQueue
ext wr : currentlist:queue wr front : element
post [front] ⃗currentlist = *currentlist*

8.14.2

stack = element*

push(new:element)
ext wr currentlist:stack
post currentlist = *currentlist* ⃗[new]

pop
ext wr currentlist:stack wr top:element
post currentlist ⃗[top] = *currentlist*

$$Concat(S_1 |: Patient^*, S_2 : Patient^*) Newlist : Patient^*$$
$$Post \ len \ Newlist \ = len \ S_1 + len \ S_2$$

8.16.2.1 $\wedge \forall j \leq len \ S_2 ; \ S_2 (j) = Newlist \ (j)$
                $\wedge \forall i \leq len \ S_1 ; \ S_1 (i) = Newlist \ (len \ S_2 + j)$

8.16.2.2

$Concat(S_1|: Patient*, S_2: Patient*)Newlist : Patient*$

$Post \ len \ Newlist \ = len \ S_1 + len \ S_2$

$\wedge \forall j \leq len \ S_1, \ len \ S_2; S_1(j) = Newlist \ (2j - 1),$

$S_2(j) = Newlist \ (2j)$

$\wedge \forall i: len \ S_1 < i \leq len \ S_2; S_2(i) = Newlist \ (len \ S_1 + i)$

$\wedge \forall i: len \ S_2 < i \leq len \ S_1; S_1(i) = Newlist \ (len \ S_2 + i)$

Bibliography

This Bibliography lists books which we have referred to in the main text, and also contains various titles which we would recommend for further reading in Formal Methods and related areas.

Cutts, G (1987) Structured Systems Analysis and Design Methodology, Blackwell Scientific..

Ford, J (1990a) Pascal by Example, NCC Blackwell.

Ford, N.J. (1990b) Computer Programming Languages: A comparative introduction, Ellis Horwood.

Gane, C (1990) Computer-Aided Software Engineering, Prentice Hall International.

Hekmatpour, S. and Ince, D. (1988) Software Prototyping, Formal Methods and VDM, Addison Wesley

Jones, C. (1990) Systematic Software Development using VDM (2 ed), Prentice Hall International.

Jones, C. and Shaw, R. (1990) Case studies in systematic software development, Prentice Hall International.

Schneider, G.M. and Bruell, S.C. (1991) Concepts in Data Structures and Software Development, West Publishing.

Sommerville, I. (1989) Software Engineering (3 ed), Addison Wesley.

Stubbs, D. and Webre, N. (1989) Data structures with abstract data types and Pascal, Brooks-Cole.

Wirth, N. (1976) Algorithms plus Data Structures equals Programs, Prentice Hall.

Programming languages used for examples

The following programming languages have been used for example programs presented in this text:

Pascal: Turbo Pascal (version 5.5), Borland International Inc. on an IBM PC AT.

Prolog: Turbo Prolog (version 1.1), Borland International Inc. on an IBM PC AT & ADA Educational Prolog (version 1.95D) on an IBM PC AT.

INDEX

ELLIS HORWOOD SERIES IN COMPUTERS AND THEIR APPLICATIONS
Series Editor: IAN CHIVERS, Senior Analyst, The Computer Centre, King's College, London, and formerly Senior Programmer and Analyst, Imperial College of Science and Technology, University of London

ELLIS HORWOOD SERIES IN COMPUTER COMMUNICATIONS AND NETWORKING
Series Editor: R.J. DEASINGTON, Principal Consultant, PA Consulting Group, Edinburgh, UK